W9-ASO-930

The Complete Beginner's Guide to Judo

The Complete Beginner's Guide to
JUDO

STUART JAMES

*with illustrations
by Robert Harford*

Doubleday & Company, Inc.   Garden City, New York

Library of Congress Catalog Card Number 76–56306

ISBN 0-385-06033-5 TRADE
0-385-06041-6 PREBOUND

Contents

The Complete Beginner's Guide to Judo

1 Introduction to Judo

Sport judo is a game. It should not be confused with karate or kung fu, which are martial arts designed to maim or disable an opponent. The object of the sport of judo is to throw an opponent of near-equal ability through the use of stealth, surprise, speed, and mental preparedness. It is a game for fun with strict rules designed to prevent injury to either opponent.

A practitioner of the sport is referred to as a "judo player," and when a player is looking for an opponent for a match he'll ask, "Would you like to play?"

There are many theories about the origins of judo. While it is generally accepted that it originated in China as a martial art thousands of years ago, a scribe in the court of the Japanese emperor Suinin recorded the introduction of a new sport called *chikara jurable* which was demonstrated to the court in 230 B.C. It was a form of wrestling that was much like ju-jitsu, the forerunner of modern sport judo.

If the origins are lost in antiquity, there is no doubt that ju-jitsu really flourished in Japan in the middle of the seventeenth century, when it was adopted by the feudal warrior class as a sport, and by the commoners, who were forbidden to carry weapons, as a method of fighting. Toward the end of the century there was a rise in banditry in Japan, a fact that made life uncomfortable and dangerous for traveling Buddhist monks, who never carried weapons, so it became a common practice for monks to be taught ju-jitsu as a method of self-defense.

With the decline of feudalism in Japan in the nineteenth century, ju-jitsu training also declined. It was almost a lost art when it was discovered by Jigoro Kano, a student at the University of Tokyo. Kano became an avid student and practitioner of the art, and as the years progressed and he became the respected Dr. Jigoro Kano, he also became an innovator of his sport. The fighting and self-defense aspects of ju-jitsu interested him less than the training disciplines. His interests became almost mystical, and he regarded the art as a method of spiritual enlightenment, a way of developing the mind and the body to a level of perfection. He selected the movements that, in his opinion, would lead students through disciplined training to this state of intellectual and spiritual sublimity, and he called it judo, which means "the gentle way." His school, the Kodokan, was opened in Tokyo in 1882 and became the most famous judo school in the world. Dr. Kano is regarded today as the father of sport judo.

Judo was imported into the United States along with the Chinese immigrants who were brought here to labor on the railroads and in the mines, but it was never popular as a sport or even as a method of self-defense among Westerners. It was regarded as strange and "oriental," a secret way of killing with the hands.

There were a few small schools operating in the United States during the thirties, but it wasn't until World War II, when combat soldiers were taught basic judo as an aid in hand-to-hand fighting, that Americans began to accept the sport and understand something about it.

With the end of the war and the migration of Japanese instructors trained at the Tokyo Kodokan, the sport of judo spread throughout the United States and the rest of the world. In 1964 judo was recognized as an Olympic sport, and although most divisions are dominated by Japanese players, a lot of the silver and bronze medals have been going to "foreigners." This is a long overdue tribute to Dr. Jigoro Kano.

The basic principle of Dr. Kano's method has to do with leverage and balance. He called it: "Maximum efficiency, minimum effort."

You never oppose strength with strength. When a person pushes you, you don't push back, you give way. If he pulls you toward him, you move toward him. This has the effect of pulling him off-balance, because he has expected you to resist. Once your opponent is off-balance, and you have carefully maintained your balance, he is easy to throw. In the same context, when you are attempting to throw, your first move is to push or pull your opponent. If you pull him, his instinct is to pull back, and when he does this, you simply step forward, apply your hold while he is off-balance and throw.

The theory of leverage applies to all judo throws. If you want to move a large object, you place a bar (the lever) under a corner of the object, put something solid under the bar (the fulcrum), and push down on the bar. With a long-enough bar you can move almost anything. In a judo throw, your body (particularly the arms and shoulders) acts as the lever and also (the hips and legs) as the fulcrum. In a hip throw, for example, the hands of the thrower are gripping the jacket of the victim. When the victim is taken off-balance, the thrower turns the victim with his hands, steps in, makes a half turn that will place his hip (the fulcrum) low on the victim's hip, then pulls hard, rolling him over the hip. This is pure leverage.

The sport becomes an interesting game when two players of equal skill are engaged in *randori*, which means "free practice." They take a grip on each other's jackets and then circle around, looking for an advantage to take the opponent off-balance. They both know what to expect and they're just waiting for one or the other to commit an error of judgment. When this happens, there is a sudden flash of movement, a yell, and one of the players is flying through the air.

It is about this time that you begin to wonder about the name "the gentle art." A body flashes into the air and lands on the mat with a sickening crash. When the victim is a small child, you catch your breath, convinced that he or she won't be able to walk for a week. But the victim rolls over and leaps to

LEVERAGE.   *The body functions as a lever in a judo throw. The hip acts as the fulcrum, the upper body, arms, and shoulder as the lever. Keeping the hip very low increases the efficiency of the lever, making it easy for a small man to throw an opponent of greatly superior size and weight.*

his feet. Like every judo student, he has been carefully taught how to land so that he won't be hurt.

But that still doesn't make the sport "gentle," and the truth is that there has always been a problem in translating the Japanese word *judo* into English. It doesn't really mean "gentle," in the soft sense of the word. You learn how to give way to aggression to gain an advantage, and this might be considered "gentle," but the truth is that judo is a rough sport. Fun, exciting, demanding . . . but rough.

THE BELT RANKS

The ability of a sport judo player is indicated by the color of the belt he wears with his uniform. The exact colors used vary somewhat from school to school. In some places you'll find belts of different shades of a color to indicate proficiency. But basically, the colors are white, yellow, orange, and green for the novice classes, brown for those of intermediate skill, and black for the skilled grades, or *dan*. A student in most schools will be tested after six weeks to see if he moves to a yellow belt. In another six weeks he can progress to the orange belt. It generally takes about a year of study to earn the green belt, and another year to progress to brown-belt status. Exchanging the brown belt for the highly coveted black belt generally requires another three years.

This, however, is not a hard and fast rule. There are students who have earned their black belts in one year, but they generally are fanatics who practice many hours a day and take lessons every day.

One thing the belt system means to the novice judo player is that he knows, if he plays with opponents of the same belt rank, he won't find himself overmatched in terms of experience.

There are many judo players who advance to the green-belt class and stay there, enjoying the fun and exercise of once-a-week judo practice without going into the more demanding skills of the brown- and black-belt classes. Dr. Kano would not have approved of this attitude, but most modern judo schools welcome it.

THE SOMEWHAT LIBERATED SPORT

In most judo classes there is no distinction drawn between male and female players: Everyone is taught together and plays together. They wear the same uniforms, and there is no need for special protective equipment for the male or the female.

Competition, however, is something else. In all contests the sexes are separated, men competing against men, women against women.

All judo competition above the local club level is sanctioned by the Amateur Athletic Union (AAU), and despite the recognized excellence of females engaged in the sport, this organization is adamant in its belief that women should not compete against men—for their own good. Olympic judo competition is even more discriminating. There is simply no classification in which women can compete.

Several women's liberation organizations are actively challenging this obvious discrimination in both judo and karate.

THE UNIFORM

The white pajamalike suit worn by judo players is called a *gi* (with the letter *g* pronounced as in the word "get"). If your local sporting goods store does not carry them, you can usually buy one from a judo school for about twenty dollars. The judo gi is different from the one used in karate in that the jacket for judo is much heavier and of a thick, rough weave. This is important, because the jacket is going to be getting a lot of rough punishment and the lightweight jacket used for karate will not take the strain.

You will want a loose fit, and it is wise to remember that the gi is imported from Japan and is not preshrunk. A few washings and it'll be softer and smaller. As worn for judo play, the gi should have the sleeves just below the elbow about two or three inches, and the legs of the drawstring trousers reaching just below the knee.

Since you play judo in bare feet, the gi, with the belt of course, is the complete uniform. No protective equipment is required for boys or girls.

Tying the belt is ritualistic, but simple. It goes around the body twice and is tied in front with a square knot.

THE IMPORTANCE OF SHOUTING

Giving a loud yell as you execute a throw is not a method of frightening your opponent. If you will go through the motions of shouting, you will notice how the muscles of your chest and stomach are automatically tensed. The yell gives you more strength, and summons the muscles into concentrated action.

Try it; you'll like it. As you make a move, any move, give out a loud "YAAAAH!" and notice the muscle action. And because you are ready, with muscles tensed, you'll find that you'll move faster and with more power.

LEARNING TO FALL

One of the most important things to learn in the very beginning is how to fall properly and break the impact of the fall. As you practice with an opponent, you're going to be hitting the deck quite a bit. This can be painful, can even inflict serious injury if you don't know what you're doing. So pay special attention to falling, and if you choose a complete novice to practice with, make certain that he, too, learns the falls.

The force of your open-palmed hand slamming onto the mat as you go down breaks the fall. There are some who contend that the slam of the palm absorbs 95 per cent of the force of the fall. We're not going to go into all the breakfalls at this point, but try one on a good thick mat to see what we're talking about.

Falling straight backwards is difficult to do. It's frightening at first, so you'll start slowly.

Sit on the mat with your legs outstretched before you. Cross your arms across your chest, fingers of the hands close together to form a palm, thumbs touching your shoulders. You're going to fall over onto your back, and as you do it, your arms will swing out and the palms will be slammed onto the mat an instant before your back hits. During this time your chin is kept pressed to your chest. This protects the head from hitting the mat. Some teachers insist that you always look at your belt during a fall. This has the same effect. Okay, try it.

You've noticed, now, that the slamming does absorb the impact of the fall.

Next, stand erect, feet together. Spread your feet about sixteen inches apart and crouch down until your buttocks are just above the mat. You're going to fall back again. Bring your arms up so your wrists are crossed at chin level, the palms ready to slam onto the mat. This time, your buttocks are going to hit first. You're going to be rolling backwards. Slam the palm down just before your back hits. And then, the moment your back touches, give a yell and kick your legs into the air. This will roll you up onto your shoulders. The palms absorb most of the impact, but the roll of the body also helps.

The old joke "It's not the fall that hurts, it's the sudden stop," definitely applies in judo. Keep the body rolling, moving with the fall, and the impact will be taken out of it.

This is just one of many falls that we'll be talking about. Practice them over and over. You can never get too good at them.

PLAYING TO WIN

Contest judo begins on the local club level after a student has been practicing for about three months.

These matches are generally arranged between clubs, but an independent student can often get involved through a local YMCA.

When a local contest is held, the judges are holders of the black-belt degree from other clubs. There are always two judges, sometimes three.

Points are scored by throwing an opponent from the standing position or by applying an immobilization hold while on the mat. The style and cleanness of the throw are important, as is the landing of the victim. If the throw is perfectly executed, the judges will award a single point. If in the opinion of the judges any portion of the throw is badly executed, they will award only a half point. If an opponent is held on his back on the mat for a full thirty seconds without being able to escape (the immobilization hold), a point is also scored. If the hold can only be maintained for twenty-five seconds, a half point is scored. There is no style or form required for the immobilization holds. It is purely and simply a matter of using strength and agility to keep your opponent flat on his back, unable to escape. Holds can be changed during the thirty seconds so long as control over the victim is constantly maintained.

A single point is required to win a match.

Stalling is a common violation among beginning contestants. The two players (opponents) are required to take the contest stance and actively try to throw each other with either a standing throw or a take-down throw. If in the judges' opinion one of the contestants is deliberately prolonging the match with merely evasive action, they can award the match to the other player as a full win.

Scissor holds (legs around with ankles crossed) on the body, neck, or head are illegal. It is also considered unfair to pick up an opponent and throw him on the mat. You cannot apply pressure by twisting the belt or use your feet in an opponent's belt. No twisting of fingers is permitted, nor pushing hands or feet into the face. The full nelson is illegal, as are hammer locks (arm twisted behind the back) and toe holds. Any act that might injure an opponent, such as falling onto your back when your opponent is holding you from behind so that he falls back and you land on him, is considered illegal.

The judges will break any illegal hold without stopping the contest, giving a warning to the offender, but if he uses an illegal hold a second time, they can award the match to his opponent.

This method of scoring is recognized by the AAU and is applied to all judo contests in the United States.

NO ROUGH STUFF

If you're going to practice judo without the supervision of an instructor, you have to be doubly careful. In any respected *dojo* (judo school or training area) all unnecessary roughness is absolutely outlawed. The instructors are adamant about it.

When the students are young boys and they're unsupervised, this rule can be difficult to enforce. They've seen judo and karate on television and in the movies and they want to emulate these experts. In their ignorance the play can get rough, and it can also be dangerous.

Make a rule right now that you and your opponent both understand that you are going to learn the moves of judo, that you are going to treat it as a sport, and that you are not going to roughhouse. If your opponent doesn't agree, find someone else.

2 Safety Rules

All body-contact sports are rough and judo is no exception, so safety rules are important.

You should never allow yourself to be thrown nor should you attempt to throw an opponent until both of you have mastered the various breakfalls. A body falling out of control can be severely damaged. Consider that the major cause of accidental death in the home is the uncontrolled fall. There is little doubt that you're going to be more careful than the person slipping on a bar of soap in the bathroom, but unless you know the breakfalls, you're still going to be hitting the floor like a sack of potatoes. And this can hurt.

Make it a rule right now. Learn the breakfalls before you throw or let yourself be thrown.

THE MAT

The surface upon which you play judo is extremely important. The mat in a dojo will be from four to six inches thick and will practically fill a large room. A popular way to create this "mat" is to build a frame and fill it with about four inches of sand, then cover this with from two to four inches of

Styrofoam, then cover the entire surface with a heavy vinyl. This gives you a surface that is firm enough for a good footing, but absorbs the shock of the most severe fall.

Since this is a permanent arrangement that would take up too much space in the average home, you'll have to settle for less than this. But don't settle for too little.

A number of used mattresses make a good mat. They're cheap and plentiful. Make sure you use the type that is without springs and cotton-filled, firm, but shock absorbent. The mattresses should be sewn together with heavy cord or sailmaker's twine. You can purchase the twine, sailmaker's needles, and a sailmaker's palm (you'll need it for this job) at any marine supply store. If the mattresses are not sewn together, it is just possible that they will slide apart during some strenuous activity, and one of the players could hit bare floor and be hurt.

Canvas stretched over the mattresses and fastened makes a better playing surface. This, however, gets expensive. A canvas tarp thirty feet by forty feet will run about a hundred dollars.

The important thing is that you do not do any throwing or falling on a hard floor. A thickly carpeted floor may suffice to practice the basic falls, but you should not use it for throwing or receiving (being thrown).

A one- or two-inch tumbling mat placed on a soft, grassy lawn makes a good outdoor practice area. The ground itself is a good shock absorber, and with the mat added it makes a fine surface. But again, don't practice any throws even on a good surface unless the receiver has learned the breakfalls.

TAPPING

In any judo school, one of the things you are taught in the first week is the importance of "tapping" for release. If your opponent has you in a hold that hurts, you simply tap him lightly with your hand and he is to release you immediately. There are no exceptions to this rule. If you should happen to be in a hold that makes it impossible for you to tap your opponent, you can tap the mat or you can even tap yourself so that he can see or hear it, and he is obligated to release you. This is universal in judo play.

If you are practicing hip throws with an opponent, for example, and you want the throw to stop as soon as you're off-balance, you tap him to indicate that you want the action to stop.

Many judo players thoroughly enjoy mat work, which is close to regular wrestling, but this is where strength and force are generally applied—and where tempers have a tendency to flare. Where one of the players is applying arm or leg locks or even choke holds, the importance of "tap for release" is greatly magnified. You must establish this rule before you begin play with an opponent, and if he fails to obey the rule or seems to get enjoyment out of hurting you, stop the practice session immediately and find yourself a new partner.

THROWING AND FALLING

As you get into practicing throws, you will be constantly reminded that it is your duty to help your partner (opponent) break his fall. You do this by maintaining a grip on the lapel or sleeve of his jacket, and just as he hits the mat you pull up with a firm, but gentle movement. This is an important movement, particularly for beginning students.

Falling or being thrown is an unnatural and disconcerting move to the beginner, and it is difficult to relax and let the body absorb the shock. Most novice players, even though they will go through the movements of the breakfall, will tense their bodies as they hit. This can be dangerous. You, as the thrower, can ease the shock by maintaining a firm hold and then pulling up to break the fall.

The most important safety precaution to keep in mind is that you want to prevent injury to your partner. This will cover just about everything. With this in mind you will be careful not to throw him off the mat, you'll release at the slightest tap, and you'll hang onto him in a throw.

Accidents happen in judo play when one of the players doesn't use his head. If you will always stop to think about what you are going to do, and what the results might be, you will automatically eliminate the cause of most accidents.

Remember that, though judo can be rough, it is still known as the "gentle way." Keep it that way. And if we seem to be preaching safety precautions throughout the book, it is only because we want to impress upon you that judo is a game, and there is no reason to be hurt as you play it.

3 Exercises

Every sport has its exercises and judo is no exception. The main difference is that in judo the exercises are not just a method of getting into perfect physical condition; they are the actual movements you will be making in throws and falls.

TOWEL EXERCISE

To make exercising interesting and useful, the first basic exercise (actually a combination of several) will teach you the movements necessary for a proper body throw.

You need a large bath towel or a good-sized piece of scrap cloth. What you're going to be doing is simulating your holds on an opponent, and the towel or cloth will be his jacket. Tie the towel at the middle with rope or stout twine. Then attach it to a wall, a stairway, or any place where it can be safely secured so that the two ends of the towel are at the height of the arms of an average opponent.

Facing the towel, grip both ends in your hands. Stand with your feet about sixteen inches apart. Your left-hand grip on the towel simulates the grip you would have on the right sleeve of his jacket. Your right-hand grip simulates the grip you would

TOWEL EXERCISE. *A towel secured at the middle simulates the jacket of an opponent. This is a helpful aid for the beginner in practicing pivots.*

have on the left lapel of his jacket. So the right hand is slightly higher than the left.

You're going to practice the movement used in a body throw. You pull with your left hand. The pull is straight back, parallel with the floor. The object is to turn the opponent slightly to the side, setting him off-balance. Along with this action, you pivot on the ball of the left foot. Your right foot glides across in front of the opponent, your body turning so that your right hip is placed in his stomach. At this point you crouch slightly to get your center of gravity below that of your opponent.

All this is done very quickly in an actual throw, but you're trying to get it smooth, so start slowly.

The pivot must be smooth. The right foot must slide across the floor. Perfect balance is absolutely vital in all judo movements, so your feet should not leave the floor. You don't step across, you slide.

As you hold the towel and then make your move, you should imagine that it is a real opponent and make your move so that your body is close and touching his. You must always have close body contact when throwing.

These are movements that you must use with a real opponent. The pull on the sleeve must be straight. The pivot is smooth as the right foot slides across. The hip is planted snugly. You're ready to pull the opponent over your back and execute the throw with ease.

Find a permanent place for the towel, anchor it securely so that you can apply considerable pull, and it will be an exercise device that you will use again and again.

In just this one throwing movement you'll be strengthening the waist and abdominal muscles, plus the biceps and shoulders.

Another use for the towel is to practice leg-throw techniques. We won't go into these throws until later, but you'll see that the towel as a simulated opponent will be helpful.

SQUATS

The squat is a simple exercise, but it is one of the best for developing great strength in the legs. It will also improve the flexibility of the knees and ankles and improve your sense of balance.

Stand erect with your feet about sixteen to eighteen inches

apart. Your arms are folded across your chest.

Bend your knees, lowering the body as far down as it will go. The posture of the back is straight up and down, and the weight of the body rests squarely on both feet. Return to the

SQUATS. *Stand erect with your feet apart. Arms can be folded across the chest or outstretched for balance. Bend your knees, back straight, lowering the body as far as it will go.*

erect position, stretching the shoulders back slightly as you do. Lower the body again, return to the erect position.

You should repeat this between ten and twenty times in the beginning. This is a popular warm-up exercise in the dojo and you'll see experts doing as many as 150 squats without taking a rest.

A variation on the squat is the one-legged squat. You do this close to a wall so you can balance yourself with one hand if necessary. Stand erect with your arms out at your sides for balance. Lift your right foot and extend it forward. You are now balanced on your left foot. Lower the body, bending the left knee and raising the right foot as you go down. Return to the erect position. Switch legs and repeat. You won't have to worry about doing too many of these. They are difficult and exhausting.

DUCK WALK

This is just an extreme variation on the squat, but it is extremely popular with serious *judoka* (judo experts).

It is good for balance training, improves the flexibility of the hips, and gives strong leg drive.

Begin at the bottom point of the squat, with the body weight squarely on both feet, the back erect, the arms folded across the chest. Now shift your weight to the left foot and

DUCK WALK.   *When you are in the squat position, you step out with one leg, then the other. You can extend the arms for balance if necessary.*

step forward with the right foot. The weight is then transferred to the right foot and the left foot moves forward. Keep this up for at least twenty yards.

An amusing sight at a dojo is a class (particularly beginners) duck-walking in single file around the perimeter of the mat. It is normally used as a warm-up exercise.

LEG STRETCH

This is another simple exercise, but it is very good for stretching the major muscles of the legs.

Stand erect with your feet spread apart. Your arms are folded across the chest unless you feel that you will need them for balance. Lower your body down on the right heel as far as

LEG STRETCH. *Stand erect with feet apart. Lower the body down onto the right foot as far as it will go, while the left leg is extended as far as possible to the side, the toes pointed. Return to erect position and repeat for the other side.*

you can go, keeping the weight of the body entirely over the right foot, which is flat on the floor, and extending your left leg to the side as far as it can go, with the toes pointed out, stretching as much as possible. Pushing with the right leg, return to the erect position. Repeat the maneuver, lowering the body onto the left heel, extending the right leg out to the side as far as it will go, and stretching. Return to the erect position. Repeat this a dozen times on each side, stretching one leg and then the other.

BACK BEND THRUST

This is an exercise that stretches and strengthens all the leg muscles, flexes the hips, and stretches the major muscles of the lower back. It will serve as a warm-up exercise throughout your judo training, even when you move into formal classes in

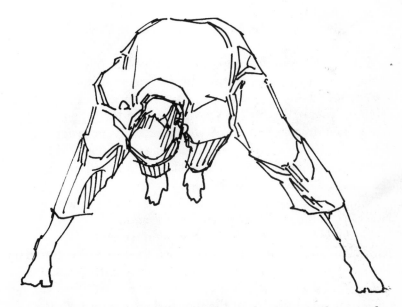

BACK BEND THRUST. *Stand with legs spread apart. Bend forward at the waist, knees rigid, bending as far as possible, and extend the arms through the legs and to the rear. Return to a position with the body bent ninety degrees at the waist. Reach down again.*

pursuit of belt degrees.

Stand erect with your legs straddled apart as far as they will go comfortably. You'll feel the muscle pull in your inner thighs. Bend forward, keeping the legs rigid, knees straight. Bending at the waist, go down as far as you can go. The arms are extended between your legs and as far behind your legs as they will go.

You don't return to the fully erect position at once, but raise the body only to the point where you are bent ninety degrees at the waist. Go down again, reaching behind the legs as far as you can. Return to the ninety-degree position. Reach down again. You'll feel the back muscles stretching. Do the movements smoothly, particularly in the beginning, to forestall the possibility of wrenching a back muscle. It is generally recommended that you do about twenty repetitions of this exercise daily. As your muscles become accustomed to the stretching, you can increase this to as many as fifty.

ANKLE WALKING AND ANKLE FLEXING

When you begin doing leg throws, the foot has to act like a "hand," and to do this it must be extremely flexible. In a leg sweep, for example, where you literally kick your opponent's feet out from under him as you throw him, the "kicking" is actually done by the bottom of your foot, not the instep or outside bone. If you could see this movement in slow motion, the foot of the thrower "grasps" the ankle of the receiver and pulls the foot to the side and off the mat.

Ankle walking and ankle flexing are designed to achieve the flexibility in the ankle necessary for this action.

Stand erect with your feet about eighteen inches apart. Your hands are loosely at your sides. Step forward with the right foot, and as you lift it, turn the foot so the outside edge is on the bottom and the sole is turned up, facing in toward the left ankle. The outside edge of the foot makes contact with the mat and you place your weight on it, trying to touch the mat with the ankle. You now step out with the left foot and repeat the maneuver. You walk this way about twenty yards, slowly

ANKLE WALKING. *Walk across the mat, stepping slowly and deliberately, and turn the ankle as much as possible until you are walking on the outer edge of the foot with the sole turned in.*

twisting each foot to get the ankle as close to the mat as possible. Walking in a pigeon-toed fashion will make this ankle walking easier.

Ankle flexing is a common exercise in all classes where the foot is used like a hand. In most classes, whether judo or karate, the students sit in a circle on the mat, one leg outstretched, the other crossed over the knee so that the foot and ankle can be manipulated by both hands.

One hand grips the ankle firmly and the other grasps the foot and rotates the ankle joint in a circular fashion, first one direction, then the other.

While you are doing this, you also flex and stretch your toes, bending them back as far as they'll go, twisting them this way and that. In a short time they'll respond as their muscles are strengthened.

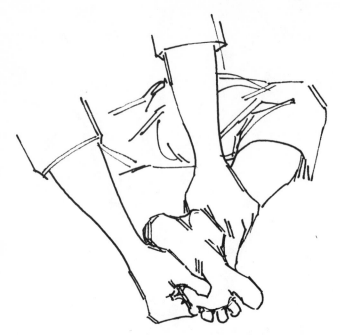

ANKLE FLEXING. *Sitting on the mat with one leg crossed over the other, take a foot in one hand and grasp the ankle with the other. Twist and turn the foot, rotating the ankle joint in a circular fashion.*

TRUNK TWISTING

You will be using your abdominal muscles in almost all the twisting, bending motions of judo, and there are many exercises to strengthen them. The old standbys common to all exercise classes—sit-ups, toe touching, leg-ups, side bends—are all good and should be practiced.

Trunk twisting strengthens the abdominal group and also includes movements you'll use in throwing.

Start with the common trunk twist as a warm-up. Stand with your feet about eighteen inches apart, your arms outstretched at shoulder height. Twist the body to the left as far as possible without moving your legs. Reverse the movement and twist the upper body as far to the right as possible. Back to the left, then to the right. You should do this at least a dozen times in each direction.

TRUNK TWISTING. *Stand erect with feet apart, arms outstretched to the sides. Twist the upper torso as far to the left as it will go, then to the right as far as it will go.*

Now you can progress to a more advanced form of trunk twist that is also more fun. You stand with your legs spread well apart and your arms spread at shoulder level. Your eyes are straight ahead and your back is erect. You're going to twist to the left as far as possible, but this time you're going to do it quickly, uttering a "Hai!" as you do it. You'll have to pivot on the balls of the feet, and your body will drop slightly as you bend the left knee. Try it.

"Hai!" The right hand is poised over the bent left knee. You're going to reverse this, now, twisting as far as possible to the right. The back is kept erect. Remember, you're going to pivot on the balls of the feet, and you'll notice that most of the pivoting will be done on the rear foot.

Stop at the end of each movement. Get ready, then make the twist quickly and smoothly. You'll also notice that your balance will improve with repetition.

ADVANCED TRUNK TWIST. *Stand erect with feet spread well apart. Twist suddenly to the left, pivoting the body on the ball of the left foot and dropping down with the left knee bent. The right leg is extended, still in position. Return to erect position and repeat the movement to the right.*

NECK TWISTS

As a prelude to this exercise, do a dozen or so neck rotations. First turn your head as far as possible to the left, holding it there a few seconds. Then face forward again, place the chin on the chest, hold it there a few seconds and raise the chin. Then turn your head as far as possible to the right and hold it. This exercise will stretch and warm the neck muscles.

When you're ready, kneel on all fours on the mat. Place your forehead on the mat. Clasp your hands behind your back and rise up on your toes, your feet spread apart. You should now resemble a tripod, your body supported at three points, the head and two feet. Push forward with your feet until you're resting on the top of your head. Twist your body from side to side, backwards and forwards, rolling on the neck.

NECK TWISTS.   *Kneel on all fours with your forehead on the mat. Fold your hands behind your back and push forward until you are on the top of your head. Twist your body from side to side and forward and backward, rolling on the neck.*

This is a strenuous exercise for the neck, so take it easy the first couple of weeks. A few minutes each day will be sufficient.

LEG PUSH

For this exercise and the two following, you will need the assistance of a partner.

Lying on your back on the mat with your arms outstretched at your sides, you lift your legs until your knees are resting on your chest and the soles of your feet are angled upwards, the feet close together.

Your partner stands facing you. His feet are about thirty-six inches apart. He grasps your ankles with his hands and leans forward, his body rigid, resting his chest on the soles of your feet.

Straighten your legs slowly, raising him. He doesn't try to resist. This is not a contest. You're only interested in his weight. Bring your knees back to the chest again, slowly. Rest a moment. Repeat the movement. Push him up, lower him back.

LEG PUSH. *Lie on your back, arms outstretched, knees brought up to your chest. A partner rests his weight on your feet, his body rigid, his hands gripping your ankles. You push up with your legs, lifting his weight, lower him, lift him, doing the movements slowly.*

Repeat this about a dozen times at first, but don't strain. You'll gradually work up to twenty or thirty repetitions as your legs develop strength.

BACK CARRY

This is an important exercise, because it involves the lifting action of the legs and also incorporates the moves used in the body throw.

You stand facing your partner. You each have your feet

BACK CARRY. *Move into position so that your back is touching the chest of your partner. You are still gripping his jacket. Pass your right arm around his waist. Crouch slightly and pull him firmly across your back, his feet off the mat. Straighten your legs, crouch, straighten, lifting and lowering his full weight.*

about eighteen inches apart. Reach out with your left hand and take a grip on his right jacket sleeve, above the elbow. Do the next move slowly. Slide your right foot to the left, turning your body as you move, pivoting on the ball of your left foot. Stop. You are now facing in the same direction as your partner, your back to his chest. He doesn't move. You're still gripping his jacket. Now, slide your left foot back and stop just inside his left foot.

Crouch slightly. Pass your right arm around your partner's waist. Pull on his sleeve and tighten the grip around his waist to pull him firmly across your back until his feet are off the ground and you are supporting all his weight.

Straighten your legs, crouch again, straighten, crouch. Repeat this five or six times at first.

Think of each movement as your feet slide on the mat and your body twists to receive the weight of the partner. Do everything in slow motion. This is an important move and you can't practice it too much.

BACK-TO-BACK CARRY

A partner is also needed for this exercise. It is an amusing, relaxing exercise that often leads to horseplay at the dojo, and a stern rebuke from the *sensei* (teacher).

Stand back-to-back with your partner, each of you with your feet about eighteen inches apart. Reach back and lock arms together at the elbows.

Bend your knees slightly, crouching until your partner's buttocks touch the small of your back. Lean forward, lifting him onto your back, and straighten your legs, lifting him clear of the mat. Holding his weight, you straighten up, lowering him to the floor.

It is then his turn to lift you. You must relax completely while he lifts you, presenting no resistance. When your feet touch the mat again, you repeat the first move, crouching and lifting.

BACK-TO-BACK CARRY. *Standing back-to-back with your partner, you both reach back and intertwine your elbows. You bend forward from the waist, lifting him off the mat and onto your back. You return to the original position, and then he performs the lifting movement. Repeat as many times as desired.*

Be careful that the lifting doesn't get too spirited. It is quite easy to catapult your partner over your head—and this could result in injury.

SLIDE STEPS

When you are performing this exercise, you may wonder whether it is serious and what beneficial effect it can possibly have.

It is true that the movements are not strenuous, but they are the movements you'll be making in judo practice, moving the feet without lifting them from the mat.

You won't need a partner for these moves, but it is a good idea to assume you are facing an opponent. If possible, do them in front of a full-length mirror. Or you can place a chair or other object on the mat to take the place of the opponent.

Stand with your right side toward the object or opponent, about three feet away, your feet in a natural stance, about eighteen inches apart, your hands resting at your sides. Turn your right foot toward the object (opponent), also turning

SLIDE STEPS.   *Stand erect, feet apart. Slide the right foot to the right. Shift weight to the right foot and slide the left foot up to approximate the original stance. Slide the left foot out. Shift the weight to that foot and slide the right up to assume the original stance. Move in any direction you like with these stylized, exaggerated movements.*

your head and upper body slightly in that direction. Shifting your weight onto your left foot, slide the right foot forward until it is just a few inches from the object. Then shift your weight to the right foot, and slide the left foot up behind the right, regaining your original stance.

Now, with your weight on the right foot again, slide the left foot back to where it was in the beginning. The left foot takes the weight, and the right foot is pulled back.

Yes, it sounds and looks too easy. It is easy, but the object is to learn a stylized way of moving. Everything is exaggerated, but you will learn grace and balance. Do it often, starting from both sides.

HOPPING

Grace and balance are the main rewards the beginner will receive from this exercise. The movements are also used in judo, but only by advanced intermediate students. Beginners keep their feet on the mat.

But do the exercise anyway. It is good for balance and timing and will add to your endurance.

You need a "home" area for this, a mark on the mat—a spot, an X, anything. The foot that supports the weight of the body will always be on this spot.

Stand with your left foot on the "home" spot and your right leg extended to the side, toes touching the mat. Hands are held at the waist.

Jump to the left, the right foot landing on "home" and taking the weight, the left leg extended to the side with the toes touching the mat. Jump back to the right, the left foot landing at "home," the right foot extended to the side.

Jump again, once more bringing the right foot to "home," supporting the weight, but this time extending the left foot forward. Another jump: The left foot takes the weight at "home," and this time the right foot is extended to the rear.

As you become proficient at this and you vary the direction of the hops and pick up speed, you can develop rhythm by

HOPPING. *Stand erect, hands on hips, feet apart. With all your weight on the left foot, extend your right leg to the side, touching the toes to the mat. Jump to the left, landing on the right foot at the spot formerly occupied by the left foot, and extend the left leg to the side, toes touching the mat, weight now on the right foot. Jump to the right, left foot landing on its original spot, the right leg extended to the right, toes touching.*

doing it to music. This is a relaxing exercise and is great for building endurance.

There are dozens of other exercises, all of them good, but if you will use the ones we have outlined here, and do at least some of them on a daily basis, you will notice the physical improvement within a month.

4 Breaking a Fall

We have already mentioned the importance of learning to fall and breaking the impact of the fall.

There was a time when judo instructors insisted that students completely master all of the variations of the breakfall before attempting a throw. This could take as long as six months, and it was a period of boring repetition until the instructor was satisfied that the student was ready to move on.

Nowadays the student novice is immediately introduced to all phases of judo. He will be learning body throws and the elements of mat work in the first week. But the importance of the breakfall is undiminished; all schools emphasize it from the beginning, and many instructors feel that it is the most important element in judo.

Under no circumstances should you attempt to throw an opponent or let anyone throw you until you have at least learned the basics of breaking a fall. It isn't difficult; it is, in fact, pleasant exercise.

BACK FALLS

We have already covered the basics of the straight backward breakfall, and we'll run through it briefly again.

You're sitting on the mat, your feet outstretched before you, your wrists crossed before your chest. Look down at your belt. This will place your chin on your chest, protecting the head, and it will also create a curve to your back. Roll back, kicking the legs up, and just before your shoulders touch the mat, slam your hands down on the mat, absorbing the impact of the fall.

Your first reaction is: What impact? All you were doing was rolling backwards. In a real situation of judo play in which your opponent is successful with a leg throw, you'll be falling backwards with considerable force. Just because judo is referred to as the "gentle way" doesn't mean that it doesn't get rough. This is a contact sport and there will be plenty of impact.

Up to now we have talked about slamming the mat with your hands. The next time you try the backward fall, you'll try something slightly different. You will slam the mat with your entire outstretched arm. Not the elbow! Not the wrist! Not any sharp part of the arm. The fingers and thumb are pressed together to form a flat palm, the arm is as rigid as possible, and as you roll back, you slam both arms onto the mat. You will find that it is the forearm and hand that actually hit because the upper arm is still off the mat, but you will also find that by

BACKWARD BREAKFALL. *Sit with legs outstretched, wrists crossed over your chest and chin on your chest. As you fall back, the arms are flung out and the palms of the hands and the forearms slam the floor a split second before the shoulders touch.*

absorbing the fall with a greater area you lessen the force (and the pain) of the impact.

There are times when you will be able to hit only with the hand. This is acceptable, but it is always more effective to hit with as much of the arm as possible.

Remember that the head never hits the mat. Yes, we've mentioned it several times, but now let's put special emphasis on this safety factor. In any fall, where there is the possibility of the head slamming onto the mat, you must take pains to see that you land with your head raised. You can accomplish this by looking at your belt as you go down, or you can just be sure that your chin is pressed against your chest. Both of these actions will keep the head off the mat.

Try the next variation of the straight backward fall. You crouch on the mat (you might call it a squat) with the buttocks touching your heels. Your wrists are crossed before your chest. Look down at your belt. Ready. Roll back, touching with your buttocks, rolling onto the curved back. Give a yell, "Haiii!" and slam down the hands and forearms just before your shoulders touch.

Do it again and follow through with the legs. The arms slam down, as before, the shoulders touch, and now keep the roll

BACKWARD BREAKFALL FROM A CROUCH. *Crouching very low, chin down and wrists crossed before your chest, fall back, hitting with the buttocks then the back, and slamming your palms and forearms down at the moment of impact.*

going by kicking the legs up. The feet and ankles come right over your head.

When you feel that you have this mastered, you can add an extra wrinkle that will turn the fall into excellent exercise and give the feeling of a free fall.

Do the fall just as before. You're in the crouch. You drop back, rolling, the arms slam down, the legs kick up and over as far as they'll go. Okay. Now swing the legs back, bending the knees. You're going to reverse the process, coming back to the original crouch. As you swing the legs to gain momentum, roll the trunk of the body forward and up. Swing your arms. Try to regain your feet in one move. Can't make it? Good. Now you're really falling backwards. Let the buttocks hit and roll. Slam the arms down, kick up the legs. Try it again! Keep the momentum going. Roll up on the shoulders and neck. Get the feet back there. Okay, now come back. Do it in one smooth movement. Kick the legs. Move! Move! Onto the feet and hold it. Can't quite make it? You're off-balance and falling back? Great! Let yourself go. Relax and roll.

You'll get this very quickly. You'll soon be landing back on your feet in perfect balance. And as soon as you do, go through the fall again—and again. The motion will become smooth and mechanical.

An important element that you're learning here is to feel comfortable and secure in a falling situation. In judo play with a partner you are going to be receiving (being thrown) as much as you will be throwing. If you are fearful of the fall, you are going to be stiff and apprehensive, and it will affect your performance. If, on the other hand, you have really practiced the falls and you know that you are not going to be hurt, you will be relaxed and confident. This is particularly important when you have advanced to freestyle play with an opponent. If you are worrying about the effects of being thrown, your style of play will be stiff and overdefensive.

Eventually you'll be doing this fall from a standing position, but stick to the crouch for the time being. Get used to all the falls before going to the standing position. Then you'll be limber, in better condition, and able to roll naturally and absorb impact.

SIDE FALLS

These falls will seem too easy, but try them and practice them, because they're important to your development.

Lying on your back on the mat, you roll over onto your left side. The left arm is stretched out at your side, palm down on the mat. Arc your right arm across until the thumb of the right hand is pointing at your chest. You are now in position to fling yourself to the right, slamming the right arm onto the mat.

There is a general rule that the more noise you make in slamming down the arm, the more impact you will absorb.

Try it. Ready, roll, slam down the arm. Okay, now come back into position on the left side. You're going to do this again, but this time you're also going to fling the left foot over the right leg and slam the sole of the left foot onto the mat at the same time the hand hits.

You're on your left side. The right arm is arced across and the thumb is pointing at your chest. The left foot is slightly ahead of the right, resting on the mat. This is all going to be done in one smooth, fast movement. The body rolls quickly to the right. The right arm arcs through the air. At the same instant the left foot is thrown up and over. The arm and the sole of the foot land together.

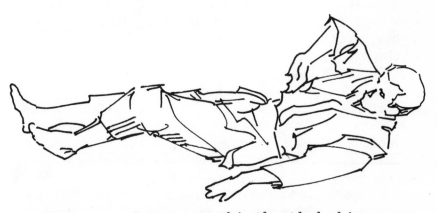

BASIC SIDE FALL. *Lying on your left side with the left arm outstretched at your side and the right arm cocked, the right hand thumb pointing at your chest, you fling yourself to the right and slam the right palm and forearm onto the mat.*

Some people do not use the foot action in this fall, but if you will try it, you will see that it does indeed absorb a good deal of impact.

Now practice this same movement from the right side. The action is exactly the same but in the opposite direction.

Throw yourself to the left, then back to the right, then back to the left. Keep this up as long as you like.

SHOULDER ROLL

This is an excellent exercise fall and you'll be using what you've just learned in the side falls.

Crouch over the mat on all fours. Your feet are spread apart, your hands close together. Your feet, in this position, will naturally be pointing out. Your hands are pointing straight ahead. Now turn the right hand halfway to the left—that is, until the fingers are pointing to the left at about a forty-five-degree angle to your body. Bring the left hand back slightly and point the fingers directly at the thumb of the right hand; then move it back from the right hand about eight inches, turning the fingers until they are pointing at the right foot. Okay, you're in position for the roll.

Note that your left elbow and your left knee are pointing in the same direction. Place your weight on your left foot and push up slightly with the right. This will throw you off-balance.

Do not do a somersault! You are not going to roll on the head or the neck. Keep the head tucked in.

Keep the left hand on the mat. The left arm, left shoulder, and your back form a kind of rocker. You will roll evenly over your left shoulder and across your back. The momentum will carry you over onto your right side, and you break the fall with your right arm and the sole of the left foot.

We've made this fall seem complicated, but this was just to make certain that you will be careful about the positioning of the hands from the very start. It is too easy for this fall to turn into a simple somersault, and that would be all wrong.

The important thing is that the left arm, left shoulder, and back (or the right arm, right shoulder, and back if you're

SHOULDER ROLL.   *You crouch on all fours, your left hand behind the
right hand, the fingers pointing to the instep of the right foot. Pushing up on the right foot and right arm will tilt the body off-balance
and onto the left shoulder. Follow through, rolling across the shoulder, and break the fall by slamming the right palm and forearm
onto the mat.*

doing it on the opposite side) form a hoop that the body is
going to roll upon. This gives you a smooth roll. Change the
position of the arm and you're going to land on the point of the
shoulder, which could be painful.

Go through the movements from both sides very slowly.
You'll see that it is quite simple.

When you see this fall done in a dojo, it is usually done from
a run. This is particularly popular with youngsters, who seem
to enjoy the tumbling aspect. They run across the mat and
seem suddenly to collapse in one direction or the other, roll
across their shoulders, and break the fall. If you could see this
in slow motion, you would see that the position of their bodies
just before the roll is exactly the same as we have described
here. In a roll to the left the body is bent over. The weight is
on the left foot, the right foot slightly in the air. The left hand
is on the mat, curved in line with the shoulder, and the right
hand is just touching for balance.

The kids make it look easy, and it is, but keep in mind that they did it slowly and carefully for several months until all the movements were automatic.

FORWARD ROLL

With this fall you'll have the feeling that you're really getting to the meat of judo. The impact is severe and you must have a decent mat. A pair of old mattresses stitched together and covered with canvas will do. This is not the sort of thing you should practice on a living-room carpet.

Stand with your feet spread apart. Crouch down, bending your knees, and place your outstretched hands flat on the mat, the fingers pointing out. Your elbows are touching the insides of your knees.

You are going to take the weight of your body on your hands, just as you would in a handstand. With your head tucked in so that it does not touch the mat, you are going to flip your body over your arms and land flat on the soles of your feet. The impact will be absorbed by the feet.

As you try it for the first time, you will probably be wise to roll on the shoulders and the curve of the back. But do not let the lower spine or the hips touch the mat. In this case, when the weight comes off your hands and is transferred to the shoulders and back, you can use the arms to absorb some of the impact.

FORWARD ROLL.   *Crouch on all fours, elbows touching the insides of your knees. Lift your body on the arms and roll forward. The head does not touch the mat. The knees are kept bent, and as you land, the soles of the feet slam onto the mat to break the fall.*

At the conclusion of this fall, only the hands, feet, and shoulders should be touching the mat.

Okay, let's run through this again. You know how to do the front somersault you did as a small child. Your hands touched the floor, then your head, and you gave a push with your feet and landed on your back. In this case you do the same thing, but your head doesn't touch. Keep your knees bent as you go over and the feet will automatically hit the mat before the rest of the body.

FORWARD SHOULDER ROLL

This is nothing more than a forward roll from a standing position that brings you back onto your feet.

Stand with your feet spread apart. Crouch down and fold your arms across the top of your head. Roll forward. You will touch first with your arms, then, in unison, with your shoulders, back, and hips. You push with your hands as you go over and come up on your feet.

You may feel as you do this that it is not a real breakfall, that you are not absorbing impact. It is a breakfall in the sense that your follow-through in the movement dissipates the force of the fall.

FORWARD SHOULDER ROLL. *From a standing crouch with your arms folded across the top of your head, your chin tucked into your chest, you throw yourself into a forward somersault with enough momentum to take you all the way over and back onto your feet.*

SIDE SPIN

This fall is a little tricky to learn, but once you master it and can do it with speed, you will never have to worry about your recovery from a throw.

Start by lying face-down on the mat, and go through the motions of an ordinary push-up, supporting the body on the hands and toes. Turn your body to the right, supporting it on the stiffened left arm, and maintaining balance with the feet. The right arm extends into the air, straight out from the shoulder. Okay, hold it there. You're in position for the spin.

Here's what you're going to do. Bending the right arm, you bring the right hand slowly down across the stomach and as far as possible around the left side. Just place your palm on your left side as though you were hugging yourself. Try it sitting in a chair just to get a feel for the movement.

Okay, the right hand is passed across the stomach to the left side and your chin is pressed against your chest.

As soon as you twist your hips to the left your body is going to go off-balance and fall, turning to the left.

For just a second you'll be falling free, and at this point the left arm is flung across to slam the mat a moment before the back hits, absorbing the impact.

Now think of it in one movement. The body is supported on a slant by the left arm and the feet. The right arm is extended out from the shoulder. Here you go. As the right hand is brought down across the stomach, the hips are twisted to the left and the left arm pushes off the mat and is flung to the left and slammed onto the mat.

The timing here is split-second, so it will appear to the viewer that the body and the arm are striking the mat at just about the same time. This will not be the case. All you need to break the impact of the fall is the split-second edge, and if you are consciously swinging the arm across to hit the mat, the body will be spinning.

Try this very slowly at first to get all the motions correct. You're going to be only about a foot off the mat, so don't worry about making a mistake and falling. You're bound to get tangled up the first few times because it is always difficult to get

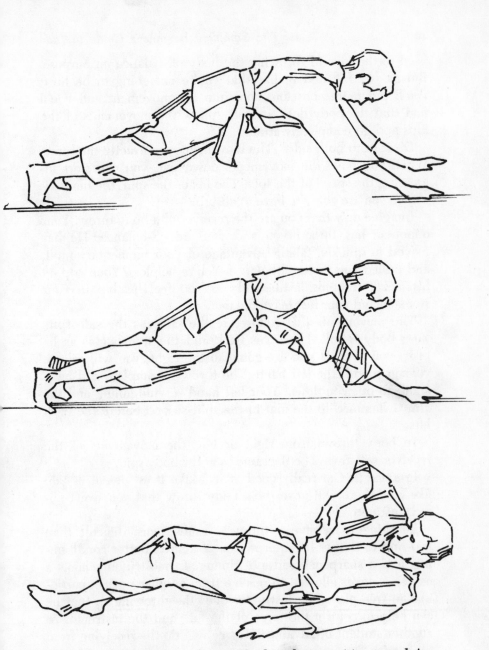

SIDE SPIN. *Starting from the standard push-up position, you bring your right arm across your stomach, the right hand reaching as far around the left side as possible. Twist your hips to the left; then spin, flinging the left arm out and back to slam the mat an instant before your back hits.*

used to the idea of throwing the body off-balance on purpose. But as you fall and realize that you're not going to be hurt, you'll put more conscious spin into the movement and you'll find that the body does, indeed, follow the movements of the hips and go completely around.

Do it from both sides. The movements are exactly the same. When you have the movements down pat, you can start increasing the speed of the spin. The faster the spin, the more violence you are going to have to absorb.

Imagine now that you are the receiver of a body throw. Your opponent has turned you and you are off-balance. He has moved in quickly, taking advantage of your momentary fault, and pulled you more off-balance. You're helpless. Your grip on his jacket tightens instinctively as you feel his hip in your stomach and your feet leave the mat.

The movements that follow are the same as the side spin. Your body is rolled over his back and the spin begins as he takes you over. If you are going to the right, you will release your grip with the left hand. The throw is complete and he is about to put you down. Your left hand is windmilling and the arm is slammed to the mat in the split second before the back hits.

In body throws from right or left, the movements of the receiver will always be the same as in the body spin.

Practice it. Get really good at it. Make it as violent as you like, and there will never be a body throw that you won't absorb instinctively.

Learning to receive a throw is much more difficult than learning to throw. It requires greater agility, better conditioning, and a sharpened sense of timing. In most judo schools a novice is never allowed to receive from another novice, particular in free play. The instructor does the throwing so that he can help to control the force of the fall, and the instructor or another student of advanced degree will do the receiving from the novice.

This is mentioned to emphasize the importance of the falls and to repeat, once again, that you should practice them over and over. If you visit a dojo, note that the black-belts, the judoka with years of experience, will still be practicing their falls.

ADVANCED FALLS

There are some falls that we have not yet mentioned for the simple reason that they are all done from the standing position and there is a danger of injury if you attempt them without supervision and a proper mat.

They are all variations of the falls we have discussed here, but the impact of the fall from the standing position will be much greater.

The straight backward fall, for example, is done by raising one foot from the standing position, crouching slightly, and dropping back until you lose balance and fall.

Side falls from standing are done by lifting one foot and swinging it across the opposite leg until you lose balance and start to fall.

When you get into a judo class will be soon enough to practice these advanced falls and you will be assured that there will be no chance of injury.

What we're trying to do here is show you the basic moves of judo, to teach you what you will need to know to advance from a white belt (novice) to the green belt (intermediate).

The falls that we have outlined are the basics taught in every judo class. If you will practice them diligently, and you must, you should be able to receive any throw or combinations of throws safely.

5 Preparation for Throwing

Body reaction, balance, leverage, deception—these are the four main factors in executing a throw.

Let's examine body reaction. If you pull against an opponent, his natural reaction is to resist the pull by pulling back. If you push against him, his reaction is to push back. To see how you can turn this natural reaction to your advantage, get a partner (anyone will do) and try this simple experiment.

Stand facing your partner. You both have your hands outstretched before you. He folds his hands, interlacing his fingers. You place both your hands over his folded hands. You are going to push down and he is going to resist. Try it. You push down and he pushes up. Okay, now, without letting your partner know you are going to do it, stop the downward pressure. His hands will fly up.

Try it the opposite way. You fold your hands and have him push down on your hands. Again, without his knowing it, cease your upward pressure. His hands will fly down.

You can transfer this principle to a throw: If you want to pull someone toward you to get him off-balance, you first push against him. He pushes back instinctively, and when you feel the pressure, you stop pushing. He is now pushing forward with nothing to resist the force, and for an instant he is moving forward completely off-balance. All you have to do now is help him along. When you apply leverage, he is completely help-less. The same holds true if you are going to throw your oppo-nent backward. You pull him toward you. He pulls back. You release. He's still going back. You move in quickly, pushing forward as you apply a leg throw. He is completely off-balance and you place him on the mat.

We purposely used the phrase "place him on the mat" in-stead of "throw," because in sport judo that's what you'll be doing. This is extremely important for beginners. When you throw an opponent, you have a firm grip on his jacket. You will release one hand during a throw, but you keep a firm grip with the other, and you use this to help break his fall. There are a few falls where this will not be possible, but for the most part you always try to *let* your opponent down onto the mat. You are not trying to hurt one another, even in competition, and judges will score points on this aspect of the follow-through.

Before you start to throw, it is important that you under-stand balance and how to break it. If you neglect this and try to negotiate a throw against an opponent who is solidly bal-anced, and try to force an advantage against him, you're going to find yourself up against an immovable force. And if he is a judo player, he will quickly take the advantage and you'll find yourself being the receiver.

Balance is easy to understand. You don't even have to go into mathematical equations. Just stand facing your partner and you can experiment for yourself.

Your partner stands naturally, hands at his side. His feet are pointing straight ahead. You're facing him, as we said. Reach up and grip the lapels of his jacket with just one finger and a thumb. Pull him toward you. He comes forward. He can't resist because he's off-balance. Push back. Hold onto him or he'll topple over. Walk around behind him. Take a hold on his jacket and pull him back. He'll topple. He can't help himself.

Try pushing and pulling him from the side. Now he's braced. All he has to do is shift weight from one foot to the other and you can't move him.

Face him again, but this time have him place one foot

behind the other. His feet are still apart, but one is farther back than the other, like a running stance. Now try to push or pull. You can't topple him because he's braced.

Now—and this is very important to your practice of judo—look at the position of his feet and decide in what direction he is off-balance. He's in the running stance with his left foot forward and the right foot behind. You're facing him and you have the lapels of his jacket bunched in your right fist. Pull him to your left. He's now like a tripod with one leg missing and he will topple. If his left foot had been in the rear and the right foot forward, you would have pulled him to your right.

Go through this with every variation you can think of. Just tell your partner to move his feet to various positions as they come to him. You have to watch the moves and think very quickly, pushing and pulling in the direction where he has the least balance.

Think of a stepladder. When it is spread out in the position of use and you push from the front or back, it cannot easily be toppled. From the side, however, it is extremely vulnerable.

If you will relate this to the stance of your partner, you will always know when he is in the most vulnerable position.

Go through the following exercise slowly at first. Then, as you get better at it, you can use it as a contest.

Start by taking the initial grip for judo play. This means that you're standing in a natural position facing your opponent. You reach up with your left hand and grasp the bottom of his right sleeve, just above the elbow. Get a good grip that feels comfortable for you. You raise your right hand and grasp the left lapel of his jacket just below his collarbone. Your thumb will be on the inside of the jacket. He takes a similar grip on your jacket. This is the basic stance for playing judo.

From this basic stance, continuing to grip each other's jackets, you move around each other, sliding your feet over the mat to take different stances, constantly on the move. Both of you are pulling and pushing, trying to find that moment when the opponent is most easily pulled off-balance.

A note of caution. Don't get too enthusiastic. When you have your partner off-balance, keep your grip on his jacket and help to bring him back to a point of balance. This exercise isn't supposed to get rough, and you'll just waste time, and learn

BALANCE. *The human body is like a tripod with one leg missing. The judo player must take advantage of foot positions that place his opponent in an unstable condition.*

nothing, by knocking each other down.

You're trying to get a feeling for balance or the lack of balance. In actual contest you'll both be moving and wary. The moment that you sense your opponent is off-balance, you have just a split second to take advantage. Use this exercise to develop speed and instinct.

When you do sense an advantage and decide to apply a throw, you have to pivot into position for the throw—and you must do it fast.

BASIC STANCE.   *The players face each other. Each takes a grip on the right sleeve of his opponent's jacket above the elbow with his left hand, and with the right hand takes a grip on the left lapel of the jacket.*

By pivoting we mean that one foot is carefully placed in position, the weight of the body is centered on that foot, and then the body turns on the ball of that foot.

Here's an example. You're standing facing your opponent. You're both in the basic play stance, gripping each other's jackets. With your weight on your right foot, slide your left foot across until it is directly in front of his left foot. If you should stop the action right here, you would be posed with your left knee bent and your left foot poised in front of your

A BASIC PIVOT. *To move quickly into throwing position, the left foot is brought across to the right and planted in front of the opponent's left foot. Weight is shifted to the left foot. The body turns (pivots) on the ball of the left foot, and the right foot is brought across and planted near the opponent's right foot, the right hip being thrust into the opponent's stomach.*

right foot, pointing toward his left foot. Now you're about to make the pivot. The left foot comes down on the mat, the weight of the body is transferred from the right to the left foot. The right foot describes an arc around the left foot, the body turning (pivoting) with the right foot. Your knees are bent, body slightly crouched. Your right foot comes to rest in front of your opponent's right foot. Now you are both facing in the same direction. Your hip is snug into his stomach and you're ready to execute the throw.

If all these right-foot, left-foot directions seem confusing, walk through the exercise just once. Do it slowly. You don't have to have a partner. Use the towel attached to the wall that you have been using for exercises. The left foot goes across, anchors, the right foot slides across, the body turning. The right foot is planted the same instant that the right hip is planted into the opponent's stomach.

In actual judo play this is one smooth, fast movement. But keep doing it slowly until every move is perfect. Speed can come later.

At this point you can also take a look at your hand positions. As you are doing the pivot, you also want to move your opponent off-balance, which you do with your arms. You pull on his left sleeve to turn his body slightly. You always make this pull parallel to the floor; that is, you pull your arm straight back, not up or down. You raise your right hand, which is holding onto his lapel. You want to bring him up on his toes. Try the pivot with the towel. You have a tight grip on his sleeve as your left foot comes across. As you pivot, you pull with the left and push up with the right. Get your buttocks down. Slam in the hip. It has to be close. There must be contact! At this moment, just as you're ready to throw, you should be pulling his right sleeve across your beltline and the hand gripping his jacket lapel should be poised above your right shoulder.

Here's another way to pivot into the same throwing position. You're facing your opponent in the standard play stance, gripping his jacket. Your right foot slides across and is planted in front of his right foot. You shift your weight to the ball of the right foot and pivot on this point. You're pulling with the left arm, pushing up with the right arm, and as you pivot on the right foot, your body turns counterclockwise, the left foot sliding back to be planted directly in front of your opponent's left foot. Your hip is tucked into his stomach. Again, this is all done with one fluid movement.

Why do you need more than one way to pivot into the same position?

For the simple reason that for just about every throw there is a countermovement to resist the throw. You're not going to

PIVOT POINT

A BASIC PIVOT. *From the basic judo stance, the right foot slides to the left and is planted in front of the opponent's right foot. The body turns (pivots) on the ball of the right foot, pushing the right hip into the opponent's stomach, as the left foot sweeps around and back.*

be concerned about this in the beginning, but as you move into freestyle judo play, your opponents are going to be watching closely to see if you telegraph your moves. If you use the same method of pivoting all the time, your opponents will catch on quickly and they'll be ready to combat every move you make.

Essentially, what you are doing with the pivot is backing into your opponent while maintaining a grip on him. The fast pivot allows you to do this so quickly that you are able to take him off-balance before he is able to perform a counter-movement.

This, essentially, is what we mean by deception in judo play.

Just as a basketball player will flick his eyes in one direction a split second before he moves in the other direction, or a boxer will feint to the left before delivering a right hook, the judo player will telegraph the moves for one throw, luring his opponent into defensive action that will make him an easy target for the throw that the player really intends to apply.

Leverage will become so natural to you as you learn the throws and practice the pivots that you won't even be thinking of it as such. But in each move, what you will be doing is placing a "fulcrum" against the object to be moved in a place that gives you leverage. You place your foot against your opponent's ankle, for example, and his own body becomes the lever as you apply pressure against his shoulders. In a hip throw, your hip is the fulcrum and your upper body and arms are the lever. You don't have to think about it as such, but the principle is there and you cannot perform a good judo throw without it.

The important thing for the moment is to get these initial pivots down until the entire action is done naturally and with blinding speed.

As you become more expert, you will be thinking in terms of a series of throws in the event that your first move doesn't work. In other words, if you try a throw and your opponent moves into a successful countermovement, you will be ready immediately to move against his counter and apply a different throw.

6 The Art of Throwing

Before getting into a description of the actual throws, it is important to repeat some of the safety precautions we mentioned earlier.

Remember to tap for release, and to release when your partner signals with a tap.

Never allow yourself to be thrown until you have practiced and mastered the basic falling techniques. Never throw your partner unless you are sure that he has learned the falls. This is important. In a real sense the body of the receiver is being catapulted through the air, flying completely out of control. Unless the receiver knows how to break the fall, the sudden stop is going to be painful and can inflict serious injury.

One other thing you should practice before you get into the techniques of throwing is balancing your partner on your back. This is very simple.

Your partner stands with his feet wide apart, his arms at his sides. You're facing him, an arm's length away. You turn to face in the same direction he is facing, and you back into him, bending your knees slightly and placing your right hip into his stomach. Place your right arm around his waist. You will have to bend your torso to the left to do this, so your body will be in the correct position. At this point your partner simply topples forward, and you use your right arm to guide him onto your right hip.

What you're trying to learn here is the position on your body where his weight rides most easily. Shift him around until you get the most comfortable position. When you have it right, you can support twice your own weight with ease.

Bring him back onto his feet and practice it again. Keep it up until you just naturally bring his weight into the proper position without thinking about it.

One last thing before we get started: You do not have to complete the throw to learn the techniques, so you can practice with a partner not schooled in breakfalls—so long as you don't go through with the complete throw. In the body throws, particularly, the important moves lead up to bringing the opponent into the position of greatest leverage (on your hip or back), and the follow-through is not necessary.

Even if your partner knows the breakfalls and you have a good mat for practice, it is a waste of time in the beginning to go through the entire fall. Your main interest is technique that will lead to speed of execution, and this has to do with the moves prior to the follow-through. You will be able to practice twice as much in the same amount of time if you stop the throw at the point of leverage and go back to the beginning and do it again.

All right, you're ready to start practicing. You have a partner to work with. The partner stands where you want him to stand, takes the stance you desire, and offers no resistance whatsoever. In the beginning you are going to walk slowly through each move. You do it in slow motion. You can even stop at each step and examine the body positions before going on to the next step. Get it down exactly right before working up speed and you won't have to unlearn a lot of mistakes later on.

BASIC HIP THROW

There are dozens of variations of the hip throw, and every dojo seems to have its own name for it. The way we're going to start practicing it, here, is sometimes called the waist throw. Whatever you call it, this is the most basic throw in judo.

You'll be using the same moves you have practiced to balance your partner's weight on your back, but now you'll be doing them with skill and style.

Stand facing your partner. He is relaxed and you take a grip on his jacket. You have his right sleeve in your left hand, his left lapel in your right hand. You both have your feet wide apart. In one movement, now, you are going to move your right foot to the left, shift weight to that foot, pivot, turning your body counterclockwise, your left foot sweeping back to be planted in front of your partner's left foot. While you are doing this, your right hand releases his lapel and your right arm encircles his waist. Stop. See where you are now.

You're crouched, knees bent. Your body is slanted to the left. Your right arm is in position to guide his body. Your left hand is pulling on his right sleeve. You're close to him, your right hip pushed into his stomach.

Think about your left hand a minute. You want your opponent off-balance a second before you execute this throw. If you pull sharply on his right side, his natural move is to shift his weight to the right foot to counter your pull. This is exactly what you want. The act of shifting weight moves him in the direction you want him to go. So, as your body is turning counterclockwise, and your right arm is sliding around his waist, you are pulling straight back with your left arm. Remember that this pull is always made parallel with the mat. The beginning judo player has a tendency to pull downward, but that will help to solidify your opponent's balance. You must pull straight back—not up, not down.

It will be easy now to move your partner onto your right hip. He's already moving forward, and you have your right arm behind him to help him along. You merely straighten your legs, and his feet will leave the floor. He is helpless and ready to be thrown.

Stop at this point unless your partner is experienced in the breakfalls. Go back, and go through these moves again and again. And keep this in mind: *Come in low, come in fast, come in close.* Speed is absolutely vital to every throw. In this case,

BASIC HIP THROW.   *Pivoting on the right foot, thrust your right hip into your opponent's stomach. At the same moment release your right-hand grip on his lapel and drop the right arm and encircle his waist. The opponent is pulled off his feet and onto the back and hip. Straighten your legs and bend low with the upper torso, continuing to pull the opponent until he rotates over your hip and is dropped to the mat on his back.*

when he shifts his weight to counter your pull, he'll be off-balance just the barest, fleeting moment, and you must press your advantage with speed. In actual contest the moment your

opponent senses your intentions, he is going to try for a countermove. When you make your counterclockwise turn, for example, you are also off-balance and momentarily vulnerable. If
you are slow and your opponent has time to react, the slightest
pull backward on his part will send you flying.

If your partner has learned the breakfalls and you feel that
you want to practice the follow-through or completion of the
throw, you continue like this:

With his weight balanced across your hip, you have
straightened your legs and his feet have left the ground.

Think of yourself as being in the center of a circle. You want
to swing your opponent around the outer rim of the circle.

Pull his right sleeve across your chest and push up and out
with your right arm. You are bent sharply at the waist. He's
going over. The moment you feel his weight leave your right
hip, you release with your right hand and, keeping a firm grip
on his sleeve with your left hand, you straighten up and step
back, pulling up with your left hand.

Pulling up on his sleeve will help to lessen the shock of the
fall and will place him onto the mat in a good position. Under
no circumstances do you release with both hands and just let
your partner fall unaided. The object is to throw him, not hurt
him.

Placing your arm around your partner's waist for this hip
throw is for beginners' practice. When you become adept at
the pivot and can move his body into position on your back
with ease, you should start using the technique that you will
use in actual judo play.

Instead of releasing your hold on your partner's lapel to
bring your arm down and around his waist, you keep a firm
grip. As you go into the pivot you push up with the right hand.
Your right elbow is thrust under his left armpit. Remember
that, as you are turning to place your back against his front,
you are pulling on his right sleeve, turning him. At the same
time, you will be pushing up with your right elbow, tilting him
to his right to keep him off-balance. You continue this movement as he goes over, and when he leaves your hip, you release
with the right hand.

ADVANCED HIP THROW. *The movements are basically the same as in the basic hip throw, but instead of placing your arm around your opponent's waist, you maintain the lapel grip. Push your right hand up, placing the right elbow into his left armpit to aid in pushing up and to the left. You are pushing him off-balance and onto your hip. You straighten your legs, bending your torso low, and your opponent is rotated over your hip and onto his back.*

You will find that with this technique all your moves will be faster.

But use the arm-around-the-waist technique until you have mastered the pivot and the throw.

SHOULDER THROW

This is another absolutely basic throw, and you use approximately the same movements as in the hip throw.

Stand facing your partner and take the standard grip on his jacket, left hand gripping his right sleeve, right hand holding his left lapel.

You'll be using the same pivot as in the hip throw. The right foot slides across and is planted just inside his right foot. You are going to pivot on the ball of your right foot, turning your body counterclockwise until you are facing in approximately the same direction, your left foot sweeping around and back and being planted in front of your partner's left foot.

So far, it's the same as the hip-throw movement. Now here is what is different.

SHOULDER THROW. *The initial pivot is the same as for the advanced hip throw, with one exception. In this throw the right elbow is thrust under the armpit of the receiver to exert upward pressure. The hips of the thrower are low. The receiver is pulled off-balance by the left hand and forced up and onto the hips by the right arm. The thrower straightens his legs, bends low at the waist, and wheels the receiver over his shoulder.*

As you make the pivot, you pull back with your left arm, taking your partner off-balance. At the same time, you force your right elbow under his right armpit and push up. Remember, now, that's the *right* armpit—not the left as in the hip throw. Try it slowly and you'll see that not only is it a natural move, it is also considerably faster to execute than the hip throw.

It helps to get your body in a good crouch, considerably lower than your partner's.

You continue to pull his right arm around your body and force upward with your right elbow. Remember that you are the center of a circle and you want to move your partner around the outer edge of the circle. Your hips should be below his. You straighten your legs, continuing the arm movements, but keeping your body sharply bent at the waist.

You can stop when you have him on your back. If you plan to go through with the complete throw, make sure that your partner has the normal grip on your uniform. This is a relatively high throw and if he maintains his grip on the lapel of your jacket, while you keep your grasp on his sleeve, it will help to break the impact of the fall. It should be noted that he slams down his left arm to complete the breakfall.

As you go through this slowly, you will see how naturally you throw your right shoulder into this throw. You come in low, the elbow sliding in under the armpit. Your buttocks are pressed against your opponent's thigh. The fulcrum is placed, the arms and shoulder supply the leverage.

To go back just a moment to the basic exercises for judo play, you can now see the value of the pivoting exercises with the towel simulating the jacket of your opponent. As you now go through the exercises with the towel, you can apply the leverage action for both the hip throw and the shoulder throw.

NECK THROW

Once again you'll be using the same pivot that was used for the hip throw.

Standing in the standard judo play stance, you slide your right foot to the left and plant it as you shift weight to the ball

NECK THROW. *The pivot is the same as for the hip throw, but in this case your right hand releases the receiver's lapel, and your right arm slides up and around his neck. In one movement the receiver is pulled onto your hip and over.*

of the right foot and sweep your left foot around and back, planting your buttocks firmly against your opponent's thigh.

Now then, while you are performing this pivot and your left arm is pulled back sharply, you release your right-hand grip on your opponent's lapel and slide your right arm up and around his neck.

You straighten your legs, taking him off his feet, and with the left hand pulling and the right arm following through, you bend very low at the waist and take him over.

This is an extremely fast throw that works particularly well against a taller opponent. If you are going to go all the way through the throw, make sure that your partner starts off with the normal grip on your uniform to help him break his fall.

BODY DROP THROW

This is a simple but extremely effective throw that takes very little effort and limited strength.

Going through it slowly, you face your partner and take the normal sleeve-lapel grip on his jacket. Slide your right foot across to stop in front of your opponent's right foot. Bring your left foot back, your body turning, until your right shoulder is pointing directly at your opponent's chest. This is the position for the execution of the throw.

You're going to pull back with your left arm and push up with your right, keeping a firm grip on sleeve and lapel.

As you pull and push with the arms, you bend your left knee, placing your weight on the left foot. At the same time, you're naturally dropping into a crouch, your right foot is extended all the way out and just to the right of your opponent's right foot. Your right ankle should be touching the outside of his right ankle.

In this position you will now be pulling him down and to the side and he will trip over your extended leg. You follow through with your arms. Again, you're going to be turning him in line with your imaginary circle. When you feel him falling, you release your right hand and keep turning him with the left. He will complete the fall on his back and break the impact with his left hand.

ANKLE SWEEP THROW

This is the first of the foot throws. It looks deceptively easy, but to do it properly and effectively requires skill and speed that can only come from hours of practice.

You will see immediately the value of the exercise where you walk on the outside edges of your feet, gradually bending to touch the ankle to the mat.

In this throw, and most of the throws that involve the feet and ankles, the foot is manipulated like a hand.

Let's walk through it. You stand facing your partner, both with your legs wide apart, both gripping the other's jacket in the normal stance.

Step back about eight inches with your right foot, pulling your partner with you. He'll have to step forward with his left foot to maintain balance. Take a step back with your left foot

BODY DROP THROW. *From the basic stance your right foot comes across to stop in front of your opponent's ankle. In the same instant you pull back with the left hand and push with the right, wheeling the opponent so that he trips over your leg. Keep the pressure on until he is thrown cleanly onto the mat.*

ANKLE SWEEP THROW. *By moving backward to bring your oppo-nent along with you, you place him in an unstable position with one foot ahead of the other. Your right foot "grips" his left ankle and sweeps it off the mat as you pull to the right with the right hand and push with the left.*

eight to ten inches. Pull him along with you. He'll have to step forward with his right foot, shifting his weight to that foot.

Ready, now, you're about to make the deceptive move that will allow you to make the throw.

Move your right foot back, as though you were continuing with your backward movement. You're still pulling him with you. But this time you are going to keep your weight on your left foot. Your right foot is moving back, but you are not going to step on it. As your partner follows you, moving forward with his left foot, there is an instant when his weight is leaving his right foot but has not been properly transferred to the left. His left foot has touched the mat, his body is shifting forward and to the left, and this is when you quickly move in with your right foot, which has been waiting for this moment. The sole of your foot takes a grip on his left ankle. Your right hand pulls down on his lapel as your left hand pushes up. With your right foot you sweep his left foot out from under him, cartwheeling him with your arms. Release with your left hand, but keep your right-hand grip and pull up gently as he falls to assist his breakfall.

All you're doing here is pulling him back with you to get his feet in position and his body off-balance, and at just the right moment you're going to use your foot like a third hand to pull his foot out from under him.

It looks easy, but if he should transfer his weight to the left foot before you make your sweep, it is going to be difficult, if not impossible to make the sweep. If you apply the sweep too soon, his weight will be on his right foot, fully balanced, and all he has to do is let you move his left foot, which is free, until you have put yourself in a position of imbalance, and then throw you.

You are going to have to do it many times to sense that moment when his weight is shifting and he is at his weakest point.

It is important to point out here that you do not *kick* his foot out from under him. There is no kicking action in this throw. It is a *sweep* with the foot. The bottom of your foot touches his ankle and takes a grip with the curve of the instep and the toes, and you sweep to the left.

There is an exercise that soccer players use that will be helpful in developing this use of the feet. You take a tennis ball and pass it back and forth between your feet. You don't kick it, but try to get a grip on it with your foot and toes and push it across the floor to the opposite foot, then pass it back. You will be surprised at how quickly you will develop skill with your feet, and you will create your own tricks for manipulating the tennis ball. A good soccer player can pick up a tennis ball with his foot and throw it.

BACKWARD KICK THROW

This is a leg throw that is easy to apply if you use speed. You are going to kick your partner's leg out from under him and topple him backwards, completing the throw with a sideward breakfall.

Stand facing your partner, legs wide apart, both of you using the sleeve-lapel hand grips.

You are going to start by tugging at his jacket to make him pull back in defense. Then you are going to take a long stride forward with your left foot, passing him, at least eighteen inches to his right, where you will plant your left foot.

Go this far with it and stop. You are now standing to his right. The heel of your left foot is to the left and behind his right heel. Taking advantage of his instinctive move to pull back, you are going to push back with both arms to keep his upper torso going in that direction.

Start the action again. As you push with your arms, your right leg swings forward past the outside of his right leg. It is the same motion as drop-kicking a football. The right leg swings to the end of the arc and then comes back with force.

He is balanced on his heels and you want to tilt him to get his weight on one point—the right heel. Pull on his right sleeve as you push up and to the left with his lapel.

Your swinging leg is coming back. Your calf is going to connect with his right calf. Your leg is straight and you want to hit his calf with force. Bend forward, now, as you keep wheeling him to the left with your arms.

Release with the right hand, but keep a firm grip on his

BACKWARD KICK THROW. *From the basic stance you step forward with the left foot. Throwing your weight against your opponent to set him off-balance, you swing your leg forward in the manner of a drop kick and then swing the leg back, slamming the calf against the calf of his right leg. Pull sharply with your left hand and wheel him off his feet.*

sleeve and pull up as he hits, breaking his fall with his left hand.

That's how it works. You pull him towards you: action. He pulls back: reaction. You step in fast, pushing in the direction he is pulling, and tilt him to his right as you kick his leg out.

Fast, fast, fast! If he anticipates your move, he has only to move his foot and turn his body to counter your throw. Once you have his weight on a single point, he'll be helpless as you apply the backward kick smartly.

MAJOR OUTER REAPING THROW

This throw is very similar to the backward kick throw and is sometimes preferred for beginners because the movements are more controlled.

You stand facing your partner, feet apart, both maintaining the standard sleeve-lapel grip.

Taking a long stride with the left foot, you step in toward your partner as you did in the previous throw. This time, however, you plant the left foot much closer to his right foot. You advance your body so that you are pushing against him with your right side.

Releasing your right-hand hold on his lapel, you slide the hand over his left shoulder and down his back, your right forearm pressing against his chest. As you do this, you pull down on his right sleeve with your left hand, and at the same time your right leg comes forward, around the outside of his right leg, the thigh of your leg making contact with the thigh of his

MAJOR OUTER REAPING THROW. *From the basic stance you step forward with the left foot, then the right, placing your right leg behind your opponent. At the same time you release the right-hand grip on the lapel, slide the right arm over the opponent's shoulder. You are now in the position to wheel him to the left, tripping him over your leg.*

right leg above the knee. You sweep back with the leg as you use your arms and body to wheel him to your left.

You simply raise your right hand as he falls, keep a firm grip on his sleeve with your left and pull up gently.

Notice, the leg action here is not a kick. In effect, your right leg is brought forward, entwined around your partner's right leg, and then swept back to bring his foot off the mat.

MINOR INNER REAPING THROW

This is a variation of the ankle sweep throw. It is easy to apply, but takes excellent timing.

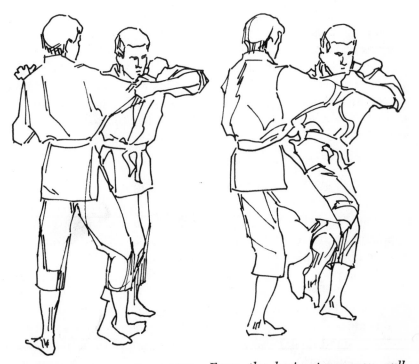

MINOR INNER REAPING THROW. *From the basic stance you pull your opponent sharply toward you and to the left. As he moves his right foot forward to regain balance, you move in quickly to place your right foot behind his right foot and sweep it forward. This is the same effect as stepping on a banana peel. You pull with your left hand and push with the right, wheeling him off-balance and onto the mat.*

Stand facing your partner, feet apart, both with the normal sleeve-lapel grip.

Step back and slightly to your left with your left foot. This will turn your body on a slight angle to your partner's. Pull with your left hand. Your weight is on your left foot. As he steps forward with his right foot to counter your pull, you reach out with your right foot, placing it behind his ankle, and sweep the foot forward. His body will react as though he has stepped on slick ice, lurching forward to regain balance, and at this time you pull hard with your left hand and push up and to the left with your right hand. This will have the effect of spinning him on his left foot.

Be careful with the follow-through on this fall. Your partner will be totally out of control and falling hard. Release with your right hand and keep a good grip with your left, pulling up as he hits.

Again, let us emphasize that you do *not* kick with your right foot. This is a sweep. You take a grip with your turned right foot just above his heel, and you sweep his foot forward. It doesn't take much because he already has the foot in forward motion.

LATERAL DASH THROW

This is another foot throw, but it also serves to bring an opponent to the mat during a contest in such a way that you have him in a position to apply an immobilization hold.

An important part of the throw is that you also go to the mat, but when you go down, you will be in total control and ready to take the advantage, whereas your partner (opponent if a contest) will be chiefly concerned with breaking his fall.

You stand facing your partner, feet apart, both in the normal sleeve-lapel grip.

Pivot slightly on the ball of your left foot, turning to the right (clockwise) so that you are facing at an angle to your partner. You will be facing his left shoulder.

Place your right foot on the instep of his left foot. You want to hold his foot there so you can trip him.

LATERAL DASH THROW. *From the basic stance turn your body slightly to the left and place your right foot on your opponent's instep. You then fall back onto the mat, pulling to the right as you go down, tripping your opponent over your foot.*

You pull him forward with both hands as you fall back, landing on the mat in a sitting position.

Keep your right foot securely on his instep. It is important that he not be able to move this foot forward to regain his balance. Your momentum is going to draw his upper torso forward and down. When he trips and is falling, you release with your left hand. Maintain a grip with your right hand just long enough to help turn his body, then release. This allows him to do a left arm roll and break the fall with his right arm.

As you release him, you continue your backward roll, rolling to the left and onto your knees. You are now in a position to bounce quickly to your feet or to move upon your opponent and apply a hold.

Practicing the straight backward breakfall will give you experience in dropping backwards onto the mat, eliminating the natural fear of falling in this direction. It should be obvious that this exercise will be a help in executing this throw.

SIDE WHEEL THROW

This is another throw where you go to the mat with your opponent, but again, you will be in control and he will not.

In this throw it is important to have your partner moving forward. You are going to fall straight back, and to avoid having him fall on top of you, you must be sure that he has enough momentum to carry him forward and over your left shoulder.

Let's try it. Stand facing your partner in the normal stance, feet apart, both of you using the sleeve-lapel grip.

Step back sharply, pulling him forward with both hands. Keep your right foot forward, leg outstretched between his legs.

Keep falling back. Pull down with your left hand and up with the right, turning him to your left so that he will trip over your outstretched right leg.

Maintain your grip with both hands in an effort to keep his shoulders off the ground as he falls. Do your best to get him into position to make a good breakfall.

When you release, you just have to roll over and you will be on your knees ready for your next move.

STOMACH THROW

This is also known as the wheel throw and the circle throw, a common throw usually taught in the first few weeks of instruction at a dojo, and always extremely popular with the younger players because it is an athletic throw and is exciting to watch.

SIDE WHEEL THROW. *From the basic stance you step backwards, giving your opponent a sharp tug. As he steps forward to keep his balance, extend your right leg slightly and place it between his legs. Now pull sharply with your left hand and push up with the right as you fall back. As he tries to keep his balance, he will trip over your extended right leg and you wheel him over your left shoulder.*

You are going to fall to the mat backward with your right foot planted in your partner's abdomen, and as you drag him forward, you will straighten your leg and fling him over your head.

Face your partner and take the basic sleeve-lapel stance. Push against him with your hands. When he pushes back, you step in with your left foot and plant it firmly on the mat between his two feet. In one smooth movement you are going to sit down close to your left heel and lift your right foot, planting it firmly in your partner's midsection, and pulling straight back with your hands at the same time.

Your partner will now be bent forward, resting on the sole of your foot.

Roll back, keeping your arms straight, and straighten your right leg.

Your partner is going to be flying through the air now. He should have his chin tucked in close to his chest. Release with

STOMACH THROW.   *From the basic stance you push against your opponent with both hands. As he pushes back, you let him come forward, place your foot on his stomach, and fall back, pulling down
with both hands and pushing up sharply with your right leg.*

your hands at the last moment and he will land on his upper back, breaking the fall with his feet and arms.

The moment you release with your hands, you roll over onto your knees and are ready for your next move.

It takes a bit of practice to execute this properly. If your foot is not planted properly, your partner will roll to the side. If you pull down with your hands, you can flip him onto your head and you'll be scrambling to get out of the way. If you release with the hands too soon, you can send him into the mat head first. Think about your moves and do it slowly a few times with your partner's full cooperation. Don't take any chances of hurting him.

The last three falls, in which the thrower intentionally drops to the mat in the execution of the throw, are known as sacrifice throws. In effect, you are sacrificing your standing position, even though you have the advantage of being in control of the situation.

We have now covered the throws that could be expected of a judo player to qualify for his green belt. In order to earn this degree you must be judged by two or more qualified judo instructors. Even though the green belt means only that you are an advanced beginner, the judges will expect genuine expertise in your knowledge and execution of the throws. Each throw must be applied with confidence and executed with gusto and finesse. It is not enough simply to throw your opponent to the mat; the form is important, as is attention to detail. You are expected, for instance, to assist your opponent with his breakfall. Your judges will downgrade you for neglecting this.

It takes about six months to earn a green belt in most judo schools. In this time your main concerns are to build yourself up physically, perfect the breakfalls, and practice the throws in an effort to develop speed. You will have plenty of time, so start slowly, go through each fall a step at a time, over and over again. Don't expect to do it right the first few times. Keep at it and you'll get it.

7 Blocking Throws

It may seem strange to teach you how to throw an opponent and then immediately show you how to block each throw, but that is also part of learning judo play.

After approximately the first month of instruction in a dojo, the student is paired off with a student of equal ability and they engage in *randori*, the Japanese name for freestyle play. They start with a polite bow to each other, then they take the normal stance for judo play, each gripping the other's jacket. After a nod to each other that they are ready to commence play, they move around the mat testing one another, pulling this way and that, each looking for the perfect moment to apply a throw.

This freestyle play makes up the bulk of the player's training. When two beginners are practicing randori, there is a lot of action, a lot of throwing. As their skills develop, the players are more wary, better at sensing an opponent's moves and countering with moves of their own. There is less throwing and more time is spent on the strategy that will lead to a throw. Like a chess game between two strong opponents, the outcome is often decided by a single error of judgment. In judo play against an aggressive and tenacious player you have only to let your guard down for a split second to find yourself being thrown.

In freestyle play the blocking is as important as the throwing and it leads to a much more challenging and exciting game.

Essentially, you can block a throw by resisting your opponent's actions or by evading the action.

To block the hip throw, for example, you can use several methods. As your opponent turns his back to you, you place the palm of your left hand against his back at waist level and push. Tilt your head back at the same time. This will make you almost impossible to throw unless he uses brute force. Another method is simply to crouch down, getting your center of gravity well below his. This destroys his leverage. A method of evasion is simply to slide off his back, and another is to quickly take a step backward. It is absolutely important to him that he maintain close body contact in making the throw.

You must also be careful in your blocking actions. If you lean backwards to resist a hip throw, for example, a fast opponent can abort his attempt at the hip throw, pivot in the opposite direction, plant his left foot, and take you down with a backward kick throw.

There are some judo players—including almost all beginners —who cannot break the habit of tensing their muscles just before attempting a throw. This habit is like sending a message. You will be able to feel it when they tense; you can let them begin their move so that you will know basically what they are going to do, then make your block or evasive action.

Let's run through a short series of moves that might be typical in a situation of freestyle play.

Your opponent attempts a hip throw. You place your hand on his waist and push. He feels your resistance and realizes that he cannot make the throw. But he is in position for a body drop throw, so he bends his left knee and shoots out his right foot. You're a thought ahead of him, so you jump over his extended leg, turning as you do. You plant your right foot on his left instep, attempting to wheel him to your right with your arms. He tries to recover, bringing his right foot forward, but it is too late. His weight has been concentrated on the single point of his left foot, which you are holding down, and you make the throw.

BLOCKING THE HIP THROW. *Placing your palm against the thrower's back at waist level before he gets you onto his hip will prevent him from making the throw.*

Remember that when you block a throw, your opponent is not going to stop and congratulate you. You must immediately try to turn your block to an advantage.

Let's say that he tries an ankle sweep on you, but you read his moves in time to shift your weight back to your right foot. As he attempts to sweep your left foot from under you, you resist for just a moment, making him apply more force, then you let your foot move freely. He'll be completely off-balance. Now it's your turn to throw. Keep him moving to his left. Step in with your left foot and plant it, shifting your weight off the right foot. Place the back of your ankle behind his left ankle, pull down hard with your right hand, and push up with the left, wheeling him off his feet.

Here is another situation. Your opponent attempts a hip throw, but the moment his back is turned to you, you squat down. He cannot make the throw. He pivots back to the original stance, facing you. Still squatting, you take the advantage and attempt a stomach throw, sitting down by your left heel and placing your right foot in his stomach area. He also squats, blocking your throw. You both come to your feet. He seizes the moment to step in on your right and bring his leg around yours to try for a major outer reaping throw, but you're well balanced, so you take a step forward with your right foot, evading the throw. You are able to pivot behind him and you release your handholds and attempt to grip him around the waist, planning to lift him off his feet and drop him. He senses your move and takes a step forward. You lurch forward to complete the waist encirclement with your arms. He drops into a crouch as you make body contact, slides his left hand up and behind your neck. You're off-balance and he throws you with a neck throw.

There are some judo schools that teach throws in combinations. Try a certain throw and if it fails, you should be in position to try the next throw. The problem with this is that the student gets locked into a certain series and it takes a long time before he is able to adapt himself quickly to unfamiliar judo play situations.

When you are engaged in freestyle play, you must be ready to meet a constantly changing threat and at the same time mount an aggressive attack. As you can see from the hypothetical situations, you can be on the attack one moment and completely vulnerable the next. You start learning the throws from a standard judo stance, but in freestyle play you will seldom find conditions that perfect. In the beginning, your freestyle moves will be clumsy. You'll be tense, often frustrated. Because you'll be thinking on the move, the execution of your throws will more than likely be late and easily blocked, and you'll probably be getting more practice in breaking falls than in making throws. But don't despair. This is a game of body contact, and it is almost as much fun receiving as it is throwing. In short order you will be adapting standard throws to a variety of conditions.

Meanwhile, practice the throws, and as you are doing it, try to envision what your partner should do to block each one.

The blocks we have mentioned so far will work against a variety of throws. Squatting, pushing against the opponent's waist, tilting your weight backwards, stepping back, turning your body. They are all simple and they work to varying degrees.

Some of the best blocks are actually counterthrows and you should learn them for contest play.

As your opponent attempts a stomach throw, for example, you grasp his raised leg with your left hand. You can do several things now. You can pull up sharply and topple him backwards, or you can hold the leg and, as you shift your weight to your left foot, step in, getting your right heel behind his left heel, and then throw him to your right.

In the event he tries a shoulder throw, you release your left-hand grip on his sleeve, drop your hand, and take a grip on his inner thigh. He has his back to you and you just take your left hand around his left leg and hold on. This should block the throw. There is an instant now when he realizes that his throw attempt is unsuccessful and must be abandoned for a return to the original stance or a move into position for another throw. At this point your opponent is mentally vulnerable. His brain is sending messages to his limbs telling them to move in different directions, and you can take advantage of this reaction time. As he pivots back to face you, you give him a push.

He should be a bit rattled that his throw has failed and his main concern is not to be trapped. He expects a countermove from you. As you push him, it will be instinctive for him, in his mental state, to push back. To further compound his confusion, you can feint with your right leg in what looks like a leg throw. As he reacts against this by coming forward, you can pivot and take him with a shoulder throw of your own.

It is extremely frustrating in the beginning of freestyle play to have all your throw attempts blocked or to find yourself the victim of a counterthrow. It is a very good idea to start off with an understanding that your freestyle partner will not block your throw attempts. You take turns in being thrower and receiver, deciding in the beginning who takes the first throw. This doesn't mean that the receiver helps to have himself thrown; he just doesn't block or resist.

Up to the point where you began freestyle play, you have been able to go through the preparatory moves of a throw slowly and painstakingly, counting off each step, meeting no resistance. Now, on the mat, moving around, you are in a different element and a simple instruction, such as *Slide your right foot to the left and plant it close to your opponent's right foot, shifting your weight to that foot as you pivot,* becomes extremely difficult to execute when your opponent's right foot keeps moving out of position. It is generally agreed by judoka that a beginner in freestyle play whose opponent engages in blocking and counterthrows will be lucky if he makes one successful throw in a hundred attempts. Needless to say, this can be disturbing.

It is exceedingly important to build up your confidence in your ability to make a throw, to prove to yourself that judo really works. There are many instructors who make a point of engaging in freestyle play with their students and not only allow them to make the throws, but assist in the throw. It is always startling to see an eight-year-old throw his 180-pound instructor and have the man fly through the air and land on the mat with a crash, but it is the instructor who is doing all the work in an effort to build confidence in a young student.

Confidence is vital in judo, and it helps if it is built up early in the game. There are serious judoka who believe firmly that things should be as tough as possible for the student. If it takes him a hundred attempts to make a successful throw, so much the better. This will weed out the insincere student who cannot stand the pressure. Those who persevere are the players who will practice five days a week, and will go on into contest judo, and earn their black belts, and maybe become champions. Jigoro Kano would be proud of them.

But judo can also be pure fun, and, particularly for the student who is learning on his own or with a novice friend, it *should* be fun and it should be pleasant.

Take your time and build up your confidence. In the end you will be just as good a judo player as the fanatic if you have the natural talent.

Work out for a few weeks with an agreement between your partner and yourself that the receiver will not make himself too available for a throw, but when the throw is applied, he will not resist or block. When you have learned to press for throws under the conditions normal to freestyle play, then you can have periods when anything goes and both of you can block and apply counterthrows whenever you have the opportunity. In this way you have the practice of applying the throws and the fun of actual competition.

There are some tips that will help in this competitive situation. You'll notice in the beginning that you and your partner are wasting a lot of energy just moving around the mat. Try staying in one place. If you stood erect and were to drop a line from each shoulder to the mat and then join these two points in a circle, you would have the area of greatest strength for you, the place where you are most in balance, where it is most difficult to move you. If you crouch down within this hypothetical circle, lowering your center of gravity, you become even more formidable. Spread your feet, place them outside the circle and you are even harder to move. Stop leaping and running around, stay in one place facing your opponent. Let him do all the moving around and save your energies for attack, blocking, and counterattack. You will learn very quickly that you can capitalize on the mistakes made by a fast-moving opponent.

Another thing to remember is that your opponent is learning

the same throws, blocks, and counterthrows that you are, and a mark of superiority is when you can come up with your own original moves and countermoves. Here's an example: It is normal to counter a hip throw with a side wheel throw. When your opponent has you on his back, you slide off to the right, swinging your right leg down and between his legs as you fall to the mat and apply the side wheel. He's going to be expecting this. Go through the motions, but be aware that he is also going to counter, and then come up with your own method of applying a different hold, something you haven't been taught, something he won't be expecting and won't react against. How do you do this? The only method is thinking about it and then using trial and error in your practice sessions. In the previous example where you are countering a hip throw with a side wheel, slow down and give him the opportunity to leap over your extended leg, and instead of falling to the mat you move in as he jumps, taking him by surprise and off-balance, and take him down with an ankle sweep.

Practice, practice, practice. This is what does it. None of these moves are difficult, but in order to do them properly and to move against an opponent who doesn't want to be thrown, you must do them as naturally as winking an eye—and just about as fast.

The material we have covered up to this point has been designed to prepare you to earn your green belt, the mark of the advanced beginner. If you have worked diligently and enjoy the sport, you should by this time seek out a dojo and continue your training under a qualified instructor. You will have to be tested in formal surroundings to have your skills recognized officially, and as you go into the more demanding throws and falls required to earn the brown belt, it will be wise to work out in the controlled atmosphere of the dojo.

If there is not a recognized dojo near your home and you prefer to continue your judo training without formal instruction, it will be difficult, but it can be done.

What you will be learning in a dojo are refinements of what we have already learned. You will develop speed, subtleties of movement, and deception. You just get better and better at the moves until they become second nature to you.

Now is a good time to find serious partners who also want to learn judo play. Contest play is important for your development, and you simply can't do this alone. The more players you can find the better it will be. You'll be testing yourself against a diversity of styles and this will enhance your own performance.

If there is a dojo nearby, however, make a point of dropping in as a spectator for a few sessions. Any dojo will be happy to let you watch. In a short time you will see the advantages of continuing in the company of other players.

8 The Black Belt

It is typical Japanese philosophy that it should be virtually impossible to achieve perfection in judo. When a student, through years of training, contests, and judging, achieves the black belt, he still has to advance through twelve degrees (*dan*) of training. He starts out as black belt, first dan, and it could take as long as a year to be promoted to second dan. It can take as long as twenty years to achieve ninth dan, and those who reach this rank have usually devoted their entire lives to the practice of judo. Only five men have ever been promoted to tenth dan, and only the Master, Jigoro Kano himself, has been elevated to twelfth dan. There is some doubt that even he would have made it to the top, except for the fact that he promoted himself.

There are three degrees (*kyu*) in the brown-belt class, and it generally takes a serious student about three years to move from green belt to brown belt, third kyu. There are exceptions, of course, the naturally talented student who trains relentlessly and earns his brown belt in one year, but this is unusual.

One of the reasons we have suggested that training toward the brown belt should be done in a qualified school is that many of the advanced moves can be dangerous unless they are practiced on large, safe mats in a controlled atmosphere.

The advanced falls, for instance, are done from the standing position.

The following are examples of what you will be expected to do in your quest for the brown belt.

ADVANCED BACKWARD FALL

With the backward breakfall you stand erect on the mat, then you arch your back, tuck your chin on your chest, and fall straight back, slamming down with both arms an instant before your shoulders hit.

This is not easy to do under the best of circumstances, but it can cause serious injury if you try it on a bare floor.

ADVANCED SIDE FALL

When you first tried a side breakfall, you were lying on your left side and you had to fling yourself over, slamming the mat with your right arm. Now you'll be doing it from the standing position.

Stand upright, relaxed, arms at your side. Take a step to the left with your left foot. As you do this, swing your right arm and leg forward. It is as though you were going to pitch a softball and kick a football at the same time. You do it with gusto. At the apex of the kick and throw, you leap into the air, bringing your left leg up to your right leg, and turn your body to the right.

If you could stop the camera right here, you would be lying on your right side in the air with your right arm in a bent position across your chest, your thumb close to your left ear.

You will land on the right thigh and buttock, slamming the right arm down to break the fall, and continuing to bring the legs across and up.

ADVANCED FORWARD FALL

From a standing start you do a complete forward flip in the air and land on your back, breaking the fall with arms and feet.

When gymnasts do a forward flip, they are expected to land on their feet, and to avoid landing on their back they practice in the beginning with a harness that holds them suspended in the air. You are expected to land on your back, and you won't have a harness to help.

Stand relaxed with hands at your side. Take a step forward and fling both arms up into the air. Spring off your right foot and swing your arms down and back as though trying to swing them in a complete circle. Your head is tucked, chin on chest. Kick your left foot into the air.

You won't be able to stop and examine your moves once you commit yourself, so make sure that you are relaxed as you fly through the air. You want to arch your back, bending your knees, so that you make a three-point landing—feet, shoulders, and arms. Do not land on the small of the back, and do not let your head hit. Relaxing is important, because your first attempt at this fall is going to be a lot like your first attempt at doing a forward flip off a diving board into a pool. As you start to spin, you will become totally disoriented and frightened, and will feel a compulsion to tense and stop the action. You will land flat on your back. In the pool this is generally unexpected, so it hurts. On the judo mat you will at least be expecting to land on your back, and you have practiced enough breakfalls to be instinctive about slamming down the arms, so it probably won't be as bad.

But there are students who "freeze" in the air when they experience this feeling of disorientation, and they can land rather hard.

If you want to try this fall, start by doing a handstand, tuck your chin, and let yourself fall. Your legs will come over in the correct position naturally, and you will get the feeling of landing and performing the breakfall.

And when you are ready to try the flip in the air, take two lengths of rope and slip them through the belt on each side.

Recruit two friends to hold onto the ropes and you have a makeshift harness that will allow you complete freedom of movement, but will save you the pain of hitting the mat totally out of control.

You can see by these examples that advancing to the brown-belt degree is going to be considerably more athletic than anything you have experienced so far. But keep in mind that you will have had many months of practice, you will have developed confidence in your skills, and you will be ready for this rugged training.

The throws that you will get into are not much different from those you will already have practiced, but your degree of expertise will have to be much greater. You will, in essence, be learning to do the same thing with greater finesse.

Let's use the body drop throw as an example. You have learned simply to turn your body as you pull your opponent off-balance, then slide your foot out and trip him over the foot. Look at the advanced form of this throw:

Standing facing your opponent in the normal judo stance, you bend your left leg at the knee and kick your foot behind and to the right, pulling down with your hands as your body turns to follow the movement of the left leg. You drop to your left knee, still pulling down, and then, with your weight on the left knee, you extend your right leg so that your ankle is on the outside of your opponent's right ankle. Pull him to your left and push up with the right arm.

In effect, you simply lift your left foot to the rear, bending your leg at the knee, and turn your body counterclockwise, pivoting on the ball of the right foot. You drop to one knee, out goes the foot, and your opponent goes down.

As you progress to brown belt, first kyu, and are working on the skills to win the black belt, you will be extremely adept at the sport, as will your opponents. Freestyle play is more demanding, the moves more original, and much of your time will be spent in contests—that is, five-minute tests of skill against ambitious judoka, each out to prove that he alone is worthy of the black belt.

It would be ridiculous even to consider black-belt training

without the guidance of a qualified instructor for the simple reason that it can be extremely dangerous.

This is when you get into strangleholds, chokes, simulated dagger thrusts, and holds and throws that can inflict injury. The fact that the novice black-belt must learn (and be tested on) the first-aid methods used to arouse an unconscious opponent indicates that strangleholds and the like are not for the beginner in judo.

But the black belt still stands as a worthy goal for the student who wants to apply himself to diligent practice.

9 Mat Work

Although it is not required to earn the green belt, mat work—
or ground work, as it is sometimes called—is now taught to the
beginner classes in most dojo.

It is akin to wrestling in that the object is to hold your opponent immobilized while you are both lying on the mat. Most of
the sacrifice throws are used to bring your opponent to the mat
so that you can apply a hold. Mat work is an important part of
contest judo because you can score a point by holding your opponent on the mat for a period of thirty seconds, and there are
some judoka who specialize in mat work to win contests.

It should be pointed out that size has a great deal to do with
success in mat work. If you are relatively small and find yourself matched against a muscular giant with the same basic
skills, stay away from mat work. Unless you are a brilliant escape artist, you won't have a chance.

You can practice mat work anywhere, but, again, we want to
emphasize the importance of tapping for release. You are
going to be grappling on the mat, applying your full strength
either to enforce or to escape a hold, and you must pay special
attention to releasing your hold the very moment your partner
indicates that he is in difficulty. This holds true not only for
practice but in freestyle play and in contest.

BASIC HOLD

This hold has a different name in every dojo, but it is simply holding your opponent to the mat on his back by applying your weight across his shoulder.

Let's say you bring him down with a side wheel. He is on his back and you are at his side. You slide your right hand across his chest and around his neck. The weight of your upper torso is on his chest. You grab his right sleeve, pulling up, and clamp his arm tightly between your body and your left arm. You are

BASIC HOLD. *The weight of your upper torso is on your opponent's chest. Your right arm is around his neck. His right arm is held tightly under your left arm, against your body. Your right knee is pressed against his shoulder.*

sitting at his side and you jam your right knee up into his shoulder.

At this point, when you have control over your opponent, the referee will announce, "Holding," and the time will begin.

If your opponent should manage to get his right arm loose, you push down on it and get it under your left leg. Put pressure on his forearm with your leg to keep the arm straight and in control.

If he should still get the arm loose, he has to lift it into the air. Push it across his body with your left hand and press down with your head, trapping the arm between your head and your right arm. He is struggling, but you are still in control, even though you have been forced to change position in the hold, and the count goes on.

If you are the victim of this basic shoulder hold, you fling your legs to the left, then kick them straight into the air as hard as you can, trying to pull your right arm under you. Keep doing this, keep wriggling and keep kicking. Start the action the moment your opponent applies the hold, making it difficult to establish the hold, and making it appear to the referee that your opponent does not have you under control.

CROSS-BODY HOLD

This is another extremely basic hold. Your opponent is on his back on the mat. You are on your knees to his right. You fling yourself across his chest, grabbing his left arm with both of your hands. Bring your knees up close. Press your left knee into his right armpit and your right knee into his side. Your body weight is pressing him down at the chest and you have your left elbow jammed into the side of his neck, your hand gripping his left arm. Your right elbow is pressed into his side. Press your head into the mat.

If your opponent reaches back to grab your uniform and tries to roll you over on your head, you extend your legs as a counterforce.

If he tries to slide out from under, put extra pressure on your knees and elbows each time he moves. You can also reach

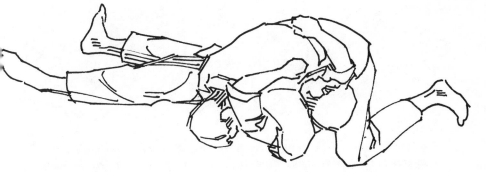

CROSS-BODY HOLD. *Your body is across your opponent's chest, knees pressed into his right side. Your left arm entraps his left arm, left elbow presses into the neck. Your right elbow is pressed into his left side.*

down with your right hand and grip him inside his right thigh, keeping your knees in tightly to maintain the pressure.

As the victim of this hold you are on the bottom and your opponent's body is across your chest. To escape, you should reach over and grasp his belt at the rear of his waist. Push and pull him to your right, exerting all the force you can muster. You also want to gain some leverage here, so try to roll your body as far as you can to the right. He will naturally oppose this force with force, and now you reverse your direction, adding your force to his, and roll him over to your left.

Keep your legs kicking and your body twisting as you work your way into this escape. Again, it makes you difficult to hold and it gives the referee the impression that the hold is not a success.

TOP BODY HOLD

This is a mobile hold that keeps you clear of your opponent's legs and makes it difficult for him to take a handhold on you, and you can also control him as he tries to kick away with his legs.

Your opponent is on his back on the mat. You come in on him toward the top of his head. You fall on top of him, your

TOP BODY HOLD.   *Coming in from opponent's head, fling your chest atop his chest. Both arms slide under his arms and you grip his belt with your hands. Your legs can be extended spread-eagled, or your knees can be drawn up close to his shoulders on either side of his head.*

head just above his waist. Your knees are brought in close against his shoulders and on either side of his head. Your hands slide under his arms and grip his belt on both sides of his waist. You press down with your head and apply force by pulling with your hands and pushing with your knees.

If you have trouble holding him, particularly if he is trying to roll you over, extend your legs spread-eagled and put your full weight on his head.

Escape from this hold can be effected if you move as soon as your opponent applies the hold, before he has a chance to get really set. Your hands and arms are free, so you reach up and around his waist and grip his belt with both hands. Kick both of your legs violently to the right as you use your arms to roll him in that direction. Again, he has to meet force with force, so he is directing his weight to the left. Reverse your action and fling your legs to the left, tugging him in the same direction. You are now combining your force with his, and you try to roll him over and escape. If you fail the first time, just keep it up until you are free or he has won a point.

These are the basic holds for mat work. There are dozens more that involve chokes, arm locks, and knee locks. All of these can be dangerous to use without supervision.

It is rather obvious from the description of these holds that mat work can be fairly rough. It's fun, but it can inflict pain and injury on a partner, and we repeat once more: TAPPING MEANS INSTANT RELEASE.

Because mat work is similar to wrestling, an opponent of superior size and strength has a definite advantage. The smaller judoka should avoid mat work whenever possible. If you find yourself the victim of a "take-down" hold, do your best to roll away from your opponent and regain your feet. If you do not have the momentum to reach your feet and your opponent is pursuing you, just get to your knees and in position to apply a hold to his legs.

10 Self-defense

Sport judo, as we have said, is not a fighting art, particularly for the novice student.

It is a total misconception to believe that, even if you have earned your green belt, you will be a match for an assailant with a knife or gun, or for a group of assailants. Your best defense will be to avoid the encounter.

In the event of a surprise attack or an attack that simply cannot be avoided, however, there are judo moves to break a hold or evade the initial attack. You will be buying yourself a few minutes' time, which might even save your life.

Since you have trained yourself in foot and leg throws, you can use the same actions for kicking. Vulnerable spots for a kick are the shins and the side of the knee. Use the edge of the sole of your shoe and deliver the blow with force. Bend your body away from the direction of the kick and it will give you added force and improve your balance and aim. A well-placed kick will deter an assailant momentarily but not stop him. If you can delay him with a shin kick and then deliver a really sharp kick to the knee, you will probably put him on the ground and give yourself time to escape. Forget about becoming the aggressor. If there is an escape route—take it!

A sharp kick to the groin will stop an assailant for as long as

five minutes, but it is difficult to apply. It is a long kick, and if
your assailant has time to react, he has only to turn his body
slightly to make your foot glance harmlessly off his hip. It is
best applied with the knee, but you must move in close to your
assailant to apply the kick, and that can be dangerous. If he
happens to be grappling with you, holding you with his arms,
then you are naturally in position for a kick to the groin. Just
drive your knee up as hard as you can. Then you can also slam
your heel down on his instep and drive your forehead into his
nose. He should release you by now, and it would be well to
leave the scene quickly. He'll recover in a few minutes and he's
going to be angry.

If an assailant grabs your wrists, you can break away easily
no matter how strong he is. The weak point of his grip is where
his thumb joins his fingers. Twist your wrist so that the sharp
inner edge is against the weak juncture and snap your hand up
to your shoulder. If he has both wrists in his grip, snap up one,
then the other. Do it quickly. It works. Try it with anyone.

But now that you have freed your wrists, you're still facing
an assailant and he's coming at you.

Deliver a kick to the shin or the knee and preferably both,
and clear out.

Suppose, however, that you miss with the kick and he gets
both of his hands on your throat.

Turn your head to the right. This moves your windpipe
away from his thumbs, making the choke ineffective. Clasp
your hands together in front of your waist and shoot the
clenched hands into the air, between his arms. This will automatically break his grip on your throat, but you must do something now to delay his attack. It is apparent that he's serious.
As you bring the clenched hands up to break the choke, concentrate on his face. Turn your hand slightly forward and
bring the double fist down on the bridge of his nose. If you are
in close enough, kick him in the groin. Or take a step back and
make another kick to the shin and knee.

Most attacks will come from the rear, which is foolish of the
assailant because this is your strongest position.

Let's say that he grabs you from behind, using both arms to
apply a stranglehold on your neck.

You turn your head toward the hand of the arm that is on your throat. This will release your windpipe, allowing you to breath. Reach up with both hands and grasp his arms. You are now using him for support and leverage. Kick back, getting him in the shin with your heel. Apply a kick with each foot, quickly, one after the other. Strain forward, bringing your head down. This will bring his face forward. Snap your head back, slamming the back of your skull into his nose. Release your hand grip on his arms, twist your body slightly to the right, and drive your elbow back into his ribs. Twist again and drive the left elbow into his ribs.

If he hasn't released you by this time, reach up and grab his arm with your left hand as you bend your knees, crouching to get below his center of gravity. Bring your right arm up in an effort to get a grip behind his neck. If he has hair, forget the neck grip and take a handful of hair. Pull him forward, straighten your legs to take his feet off the ground, and throw him over your shoulders. Put him down as hard as you can and then clear out. After this display of resistance it will take an extremely tenacious assailant to pursue the fight.

In the event of an attack with a club from the front or side, you face the swinging arm and raise both of your fists together to block his forearm with both of your forearms. This will stop the blow or at least lessen the impact. But it is not going to stop him from swinging again.

Having blocked the blow with your forearms, it is important to get a hold on the club arm. Use any grip that is convenient. Then you can use the arm for leverage and deliver a kick to his knee.

The most natural thing to do at this point, assuming that you have been practicing your basic throws, will be to pivot in and put him down with a shoulder throw.

Again, do not try to become the aggressor. These moves will help you to buy time. A black-belt, fifth dan, could mount a fearsome attack because he is trained in these areas, but as a novice you will be endangering yourself to assume that you can overpower a serious assailant.

Most physical threats against you will not come from an assailant planning serious injury or robbery, but from a bully who is merely asserting himself. This can be an unpleasant experience, but it rarely calls for the type of defenses we have just outlined. The bully seldom wants to mix into a situation where the outcome is doubtful, and if you can convince him that he is in for a difficult fight, he'll usually back off with a show of bravado.

A typical confrontation starts with posturing and verbal threats. Stand facing the aggressor with your hands at your sides, relaxed and unthreatening, but ready. Don't bother answering his threats, but make it plain by your demeanor that you don't fear him. If your hands are shaking and your insides are tumbling about, try a quiet smile.

You are waiting for him to make a move with his hands, a fighting gesture. But you want to concentrate on the position of his right leg. That knee is going to be your target.

The moment he raises his hands in the boxer's stance or makes any physically threatening gesture, you spring into action.

Your left foot slides a foot to the left, knees slightly bent, giving you the typical stance for judo play. You shoot your right arm out, your hand in a stiff-fingered posture directed at his face. This is all in one movement and is accompanied by as bloodcurdling a yell as you can manage. You don't touch him with the extended hand. This whole movement is just to convince him that he has foolishly tangled with a ninth-dan black-belt. He should be startled enough to recoil in defense, and this is when you pivot on your left foot, bending at the waist to deliver a right-foot kick to his right knee. Don't stop here. Step right in with a long stride with your left foot—the same move you would make for the major outer reaping throw. You come in on his right side, getting a hold on him so that your right arm is across his chest, get your right leg behind him, and throw him backwards.

Take a step back and wait. His leg hurts. His vanity has been wounded, but, most important for you, he has seen enough television to imagine that you are some kind of kung fu expert, and you clearly have the advantage. The fight should stop here, but even if he pursues it out of a sense of pride, he will be so wary that he will be totally ineffective.

These self-defense moves are not part of the regular training for sport judo and they have no place in the normal dojo.

Practice them if it gives you a feeling of confidence in yourself, but never deliver kicks or blows to a partner. These are moves that you should use only when your life or safety is in jeopardy.

11 Finding a Good Judo School

The ideal place for a student to train is a good dojo with excellent instructors and serious students.

Finding such a place is not all that easy, but there are some guidelines that you can follow.

Visit the school and talk to the manager. Ask about the instructors. What are their belt ranks? Are they ranked with the International Judo Federation? Have they studied at the Tokyo Kodokan? Most of the really good instructors, even Americans and Europeans, have spent some time there. The Kodokan is stringent in its requirements.

Look over the facility, but don't be taken in by saunas and glittering exercise rooms. The best judo schools in New York City, for example, are in dingy lofts. Ask about the mat. Why is it so hard? Why not make it thicker? If the manager knows what he's talking about, he'll tell you that a soft mat can result in broken ankles. It must be firm.

Attend a class and see what they're teaching. The ideal school is a combination of detailed instruction and freestyle play. If they concentrate on one without the other, you are going to suffer as a student. Attend both a children's and adult's class, and at the adult class ask a player of advanced degree what he thinks of the school. They're usually rather outspoken.

Does the school engage in competitions? Even if you don't care to compete for trophies and advanced degrees yourself, you will find better instruction and a better attitude in a school that does.

How many lessons a week do they suggest? Most judo instructors want their students to take at least two lessons a week, with the lessons lasting one hour. If you have to miss a lesson, they'll want you to make it up in the following week.

There is a great deal of variation in the cost of instruction, but beware of schools that offer large discounts for long-term contracts. Most good schools will want you to sign up for at least four months. The charge for this will be about $120. You will receive two lessons a week, but most of the good schools will also make it known that you are welcome to come to the dojo and play whenever they're open.

STARTING A CLUB

If you find yourself in an area where there is not a dojo within reasonable driving distance and you are seriously interested in judo training, you can establish your own dojo.

The first step in this direction is to form a judo club. You can advertise in the local newspaper and post notices on the bulletin boards of schools, YMCAs and YWCAs, corporate offices, grocery stores—anywhere that they can be seen and read by a diverse cross section of your community. Simply say that you are forming a judo club for the purpose of learning and practicing judo, stressing the fact that all will be beginners, and give a time and place for the initial meeting.

It is a rather good idea before your first meeting to have some answers to the basic problems you will be facing as a club:

The location of the dojo. This must be a large room. It can be a manufacturing loft that is vacant and for rent. It can be a storefront or an office location. It can also be a church basement, a youth club, the YMCA, any place that you are able to secure the room to place your mat. If the facility has a dressing room and showers, so much the better, but they are not a necessity.

The mat. This is the most important piece of equipment that you will require. You want it large, thick (four to six inches), and stable. It has to be soft, but not too soft. You can use a number of hair mattresses, double thickness, and sewn together. They are held in place by a wooden frame and covered with vinyl or canvas.

The sensei. The services of a qualified black-belt instructor will add greatly to the quality of your training and will more than double the speed of your progress. Perhaps there is a black-belt in your area who will offer his services, or you might be able to hire the services of an instructor from a nearby city. A judo club in Stamford, Connecticut, has a Japanese sensei trained at the Tokyo Kodokan who travels out from New York City (a one-hour train ride) two nights a week.

The costs. Your membership fees will have to cover the costs of the dojo, the mat, and the sensei; and if you have an idea in advance what everything is likely to cost, you'll have something to start with at the first meeting.

You should open your first meeting with a statement of what you think the aims of the club should be, state the problems and possible solutions, then open the meeting to discussion. It is very likely that among the people who have assembled in answer to your announcements there will be some who can solve some of the problems. Someone might be able to contribute the space for the dojo, someone else a warehouseful of mattresses, and one of them might be a black-belt looking for the company of other enthusiasts, and he could take over as instructor.

Beyond this, your club is like any hobby club. You'll need officers and workers, by-laws and rules, a treasurer and a bank account. But this will proceed naturally if you have a good turnout at your first meeting.

The advantage of forming a judo club is the possibility of membership in state and national judo organizations for the purpose of having your degrees officially recognized and the challenge of sanctioned contests with other clubs.

There are national judo organizations that promote the sport, maintain the quality of instruction, and give recognition to the belt degrees. The United States Judo Association, 6417

Manchester Avenue, St. Louis, Missouri 63139, can offer names and addresses of local judo clubs, and when you become a member you receive schedules of competitive events.

The Amateur Athletic Union, 3400 West 86th Street, Indianapolis, Indiana 46268, is the governing body for all judo competition on the state and national level. Anyone can be a member of the AAU (three-dollar annual membership), and for your membership fee you will receive their handbook, which outlines in detail all the rules and regulations relative to contest judo.

Judo Terminology

Wherever you play judo, in whatever town, state, or country, you will find that the language of judo is Japanese. We have used a few key terms but have held to English for the most part to avoid confusing the student. There are some common words and phrases, however, that you will hear used in just about every dojo, and we will give you a sampling of them with their English translations.

Ashiwaza   Techniques for foot throws
Atemi   Blows taught to black-belts
Dan   Degrees or teaching grades for black-belts
Dojo   School, a place where judo is practiced
Hajime   Signal from referee to start a contest
Ippon   A point won in a contest
Judo   The way, the easy way, the gentle way, the natural way
Judogi (gi)   The uniform worn for judo play
Judoka   Judo man, student, practitioner of judo
Kake   Application of a throw
Kata   The forms, the formal movements
Katamewaza   Mat work, ground work
Kyu   Teaching grades from white belt through the three degrees of brown belt
Nagewaza   Techniques used for throwing

Randori   Free play or freestyle play
Sensei   The teacher, the master
Shiai   Contest
Ukemiwaza   The art of breaking falls
Yuseigachi   A referee's decision

INDEX

STUART JAMES is a professional writer with a love of participation sports. Besides holding a green belt in sport judo, he is a certified scuba diver, a pilot, and a sailor. For six years he was a writer/editor for *Popular Mechanics* magazine. His main interests at the moment are his children (all outdoor enthusiasts) and a thirty-eight-foot Tahiti ketch that is being outfitted to cross the Atlantic.